MW00957626

# Until Italy

## A Traveler's Memoir

Debra VanDeventer

Copyright © 2024 Debra VanDeventer

All rights reserved. Use of any part of this publication without prior written consent of the publisher is an infringement of the copyright law.

*Until Italy* is a work of creative nonfiction. Some names and identifying details have been changed.

# Dedication

To Ed, forever my leading man.

And to my supporting cast, the real Anne and Scott.

*"In life it's not where you go—it's who you travel with."*
*~ Charles Schulz*

# Prologue
## The Bubble

Too bold. 'Cajun Shrimp' would be more at home in a restaurant than in a nail salon. I return the vibrant orangey-red polish to the rack and move to milder tones.

"Pick your color, please."

The technician is impatient. He has already lined the foot bath with blue plastic—a post-COVID invention that resembles an oversized shower cap—and is filling the basin with water. Clients in various stages of the pedicure process sit along one wall of the salon. Their upper bodies jiggle in massage chairs while they engage with their phones and soak their feet in tepid water. Electric files buzz at the manicure stations as patrons offer their hands to masked professionals who grind away old lacquer. The fragile nails undergo amazing transformation as armored coats of color render them glamorous and indestructible.

My attendant motions towards a chair. Chemical smells envelop me, creating a lack of judgment, or perhaps a moment of inspiration. Grabbing 'Cajun Shrimp,' I follow the man to my designated station. I place my phone and iced chai latte on the tray, and slip off my sandals before relaxing into my spa experience.

Only I'm not relaxed. The water is baby-bath warm and the plastic liner is slick and bunchy under my feet. Thinking a massage might help, I press random buttons on the remote control and the chair comes alive. I have a choice between a wave motion that runs up and down my back, or a thumping between my shoulder blades. Neither is pleasant. I turn off the massager, pick up my phone and scroll through my Facebook, check emails, and make notes in my on-line journal for future blog posts or stories. The technician signals for me to take one foot out of the water. He snips, files, and digs at my cuticles. I flinch when he hits a sensitive spot. I'm not a regular pedicure client; this is a special occasion.

My birthday is tomorrow.

There, I said it, just to myself. In less than twenty-four hours, I begin a new decade. I've never paid much attention to my chronological age. My philosophy has always been to enjoy life wherever I am on the spectrum of birth to death, but the number attached to this birthday seems huge, heavy, monumental. I imagine a number line and I can clearly see that there are more numbers behind me than ahead of me. I've come to the stark realization that my time is finite, but rather than being morbid about it—*poor me, I'm old*—a sense of urgency arises. My life story isn't finished and I can't afford to let my remaining days pass by, one after the other, in a blur.

My other foot comes out of the water.

"Cut them short?" the nail technician asks.

"Yes, I'm going to Italy next week and I'll be doing a lot of walking."

This is the other reason for today's visit. The man pats my feet dry, applies the clear base coat, and paints a sample toe.

"You like?" he asks rather tentatively.

I look up from my phone. The Cajun Shrimp toe startles me. I should have picked something more subtle and within the theme of my Italian vacation like Strawberry Gelato, or Tuscan Sunrise, but not wanting to go through the whole decision process again, I stand by my choice.

"Yes, fine," I nod.

One by one, the other toes turn bright. The technician gingerly positions my freshly painted digits into the toe-separator, slips my feet into floppy foam sandals, and escorts me to the nail drying machine. I put my feet under the warm, circulating air and glance down again at my toes. With all ten painted, the effect is less alarming, I think.

"Picking out the color is the hardest part," I joke to the lady next to me.

"That's why I always stick with a color in the same tone," she replies. "Once, I tried to do something different. When I came home with turquoise toes, my husband just rolled his eyes."

I don't tell her I'd had turquoise toes once.

"Is this your usual nail salon?" she asks.

"I'm not a regular, but I've been here several times. They do a pretty good job and the prices are reasonable," I respond. "Are you new to the area?"

"Not really. My husband and I retired and moved here several years ago. We live in Sunset Ranch."

"Oh, that's a nice place," I say. "My husband and I looked into some of those 55-and-over active adult communities, but we decided on a... (I pause, searching for the right word. Multi-generational? Family friendly? Inclusive? Age-diverse? I settle on) *regular* neighborhood. We didn't want to be tied down to high HOAs." Knowing that wasn't our only reason, I opted to frame the decision as a financial one.

"Well, the HOAs can be a little much, but the amenities are worth it, and it is *gated*," my pedicure partner continues. "We hardly need our car anymore. We drive our cart to the golf course or pool, or restaurants. We seldom leave—just once a week to get groceries or run errands. My husband calls the Ranch our Bubble." She gives a small laugh.

I think back to last week when I visited my friend at an 'active-adult' community. She asked me to join her for lunch and a swim to celebrate my birthday and upcoming trip. At the activity center, the extravagant pool area offered a breathtaking view of the mountains. While my friend swiped us in, I noticed the sign on the gate showed this was an "adults only" pool—children were only allowed at certain times. We swam a bit, then settled back in the luxurious pool-side chaise lounges.

A group of women gathered in the center of the pool with various types of floatation devices. They wore sensible swimsuits and wide-brimmed hats. Made-up faces and oversized sunglasses led me to believe these ladies would not be dunking their heads. Their arms and legs moved leisurely underwater while they chatted away.

"I could get used to this," I purred to my friend as the Bubble seduced me.

A few days later, I told my realtor I might consider moving to this type of community after all.

"You're not ready for that," she joked.

Perhaps she was right, yet haven't I made my own type of Bubble? After retiring, my husband and I settled into a comfortable routine. There is no need to set the alarm. Each morning we rise with the sun and go for a walk, followed by a leisurely breakfast. We plan out our meals a week in advance, make a grocery list, and shop on Wednesdays. Monday is laundry day; Saturday is house cleaning and we eat lunch (at the same sandwich shop) on Wednesdays and Saturdays.

Like the retired teacher I am, I fill in the blanks on my calendar, scheduling time to write, work on a sewing project or meet friends for lunch or coffee. We plan regular visits with our children and grandchildren and since retiring we have traveled to England and Italy. Both Ed and I are in good health. There is nothing to complain about. I could live out the rest of the years on my number line like this—my arms and legs moving placidly under the surface, keeping me afloat as I drift away...

Suddenly, I'm suffocated by the Bubble I'd unwittingly created. Maybe, even for a short while, I want to ditch my routine and wake up with a sense of 'what if' rather than 'I already know what today will bring,' get a little lost, shake things up and make some waves.

The toe-dryer shuts off, snapping me back to the salon. I pay my bill, leaving a generous tip in honor of my bold Cajun Shrimp toes that now seem the perfect start to my new decade. I can't wait until Italy.

# Sorrento, Pompeii, and the Amalfi Coast

*Italy is a dream that keeps returning
for the rest of your life.*
*~ Anna Akhmatova*

# Fly Away
*Vola Via*

It's 3 am. Our bags are in the trunk of our older car because we don't want to leave the newer car at the airport. Ed puts the key in the ignition and turns. Nothing. He tries again. Still nothing. The twenty-year-old Saturn ran perfectly yesterday when we took her for a test drive. We even ran her through the car wash and filled her with gas, but apparently she doesn't *want* to wake up in the middle of the night only to be abandoned at the *Park and Fly* while the new Honda CRV gets to vacation in our garage. Ed and I look at each other. We are half asleep and have a plane to catch. Without saying a word, we load our luggage into the car that we *didn't* want to leave at the airport for three weeks. The stars are brilliant in the clear Tucson sky as we drive over dark, deserted streets.

"Do you think Anne and Scott have left Indianapolis yet?" I ask Ed.

He glances at the dashboard clock. "Factoring in the time difference, they should have." According to our plans they will arrive in Atlanta a few hours before us. We'll have enough time to meet up and

9

grab some food before we all get on the ten-hour flight to Rome.

Ed and I are traveling with our close friends, Anne and Scott, who we met while teaching in Indiana. The first connection was Ed and Anne's. They worked in the science department at the same high school. Anne's husband Scott taught English at the rival high school in town and I taught kindergarten, which immediately cast me as the hands-down winner of "best classroom stories told around the dinner table." Our foursome started hanging out together outside of school and discovered we had a lot in common. Though we didn't know each other at the time, we grew up in the same town and share similar histories. The connection to our friends remained close after Ed and I retired to Arizona, and we've discovered we are good travel companions. It's a rare gift to find people you can travel with and remain friends. We jokingly attribute our success to two words: separate bathrooms.

This is the third European trip we've done together and it will be our second visit to Italy. The first one to Milan, Florence, Venice, and Rome occurred right before the pandemic of 2020 shut down the country, then the rest of the world. We fell in love with Italy, and three years later, as travel restrictions relax, we are eager to start out again. This time we will tour southern Italy and Sicily.

We've been mapping out our agenda for almost a year during online happy hour sessions. With the help of a travel agent, we booked our lodging, planes, trains, boats, and private day trips, avoiding any packaged tours or large-group travel experiences. We like the challenge of traveling on our own. The ups and downs, the highs and lows, the opportunities and the challenges all weave themselves into the unique landscape of each trip we have taken together.

I enjoy the planning stage, where we think about what each of us wants to do and see, and come up with a trip agenda tailor-made for us. I've often wondered if this personality trait is in my DNA and that's why being a teacher was a perfect career choice. Or was it that thirty-plus years in the elementary classroom created this part of me? Maybe a bit of both, but at any rate, this side of my brain was in full force as we mapped out our trip.

Months before departure day, Anne and I focused on our wardrobes. This is important because we will travel for over two weeks with only our carry-on bags, and our clothing needs to be practical. We texted back and forth, often sending pictures of various choices:

"What about these capris?"

"Looks good, I'm bringing these slacks."

"How many pairs of underwear?"

"A week's worth, we can do laundry in the sink."

"Tennis shoes? Sandals?"

"Both."

"Are you bringing an umbrella?"

"No."

"Well, I am."

Our husbands, on the other hand, never discuss their wardrobes with each other. Ed starts a few days before we leave and packs his standard travel attire: two pair of Columbia travel pants, five shirts (mostly versions of his favorite blue short-sleeved one), socks, underwear, and hat (he's sun-sensitive). For Scott, its two pairs of jeans, polo shirts–that he saves for travel–and cowboy boots. I'm assuming he's packed a sufficient supply of socks and underwear, but you know...too much information.

In the end, I decide on a simple wardrobe of basic black pants with a variety of tops, a bathing suit, undies, socks, a rain jacket, a light sweater, walking shoes, sandals, and a travel umbrella. At my daughter's insistence, I'm bringing a small pharmacy: antacids, Pepto-Bismol, throat lozenges, ibuprofen, cold and sinus tablets, Neosporin, Band-Aids, a thermometer, and face masks (they are required on trains in Italy). I think this arsenal is unnecessary, but "Mom, it's a post-COVID world. You never know what you might be exposed to," she warned.

Besides our carry-ons, Anne and I each have a small "emergency" bag we will have with us on the plane in case our checked bags get lost. These hold a folder containing all our reservations, vouchers, a detailed itinerary, a change of clothing, and essential medications. We've thought of everything. If our plane goes down over the Atlantic Ocean, we'll grab these bags after we put on our life vests. At least on the life raft, we will have a change of clothes, blood pressure meds, and our itinerary.

Planner-Me is ready. But now that we are almost to the airport and it's too late to change anything, Worry-Warrior Me pipes up. I'm not surprised, but I was hoping she wouldn't come along on this trip. Her nags taunt me from the backseat:

*Your feet are going to swell up on the plane. You should have worn compression socks instead of those special "no-show" socks you bought so you would look cute in your sneakers. And what if your plane to Atlanta is delayed, or even worse— canceled, and you miss your connection and Anne and Scott will go on to Rome without you? Then you may never find each other and the itinerary won't work and the trip will be ruined. Oh, by the way, did you remember to put the garage door down?*

I close my eyes and try to block her out.

The sparsely populated Tucson Airport is just waking up when Ed and I walk to the kiosk to check our carry-ons. I place my bag on the scale and am not surprised that it is well under the weight limit. I feel superior to those poor souls dragging pieces of baggage large enough to hold a body. Obviously, they did not consult the travel experts when packing. The attendant attaches labels, and our luggage disappears through the portal, vanishing into the great unknown.

A quick jaunt through security, our passports are in order, and before long, we are on our way. I close my eyes and entrust the travel gods to make sure we, and our baggage, get from Tucson to Atlanta to Rome, on time and in one piece. As the plane accelerates down the runway towards the sunrise, the engines roar and I am pushed back into my seat. With the plane's last shudder, I leave familiar ground behind.

# Arrival

*Arrivio*

Our plane touches down in Rome after what seems like a week in transit. In my current state, I don't possess the mental aptitude to calculate how many hours it's been since we awoke this morning (yesterday morning?) in Tucson. We've been flying towards the next day and time has lost all meaning.

Once we have our luggage, I want to visit a real bathroom, not the closet-sized one I've been using on the plane with the toilet that slurps everything into a blue swirl of chemicals and sends it who knows where. I grab my cosmetic bag and join a long queue of women who have the same thought. After taking care of my most urgent needs, I go to the sink and brush the taste of airplane food and night-breath off my teeth. The back of my pixie-cut hair is sticking out in strange directions from attempting to sleep sitting up, and I give it a splash of water and a quick comb out. My yoga pants, tee shirt, and cardigan outfit has served me well as a combination of casual wear and travel pajamas, but we still have a long way to go. I put on a swipe of lipstick, emerging slightly refreshed with high expectations.

"What took you so long? Did you take a shower?" Ed jokes, noticing my damp hair.

On our previous trip to Italy, we'd spent several days in Rome. This time we are only passing through. A train will take us to Naples, then we have arranged for a driver to route us to Sorrento, our first destination. After a few false starts, we find the train terminal and Anne and Ed approach the ticket counter, leaving Scott and I to wait with the luggage. Scott loves traveling, but gets nervous on planes. I can tell he's glad to have his feet planted on the ground.

I glance towards Ed and Anne at the window and see the agent point towards the other end of the station.

"This can't be good," Scott says as Ed and Anne return.

"What's wrong? Didn't our tickets go through?" I ask.

"Everything's fine, but we need to take a commuter train from the airport to the Roma Central Station. That's where we catch the train to Naples," Anne says.

Scott sighs.

"It's fine," she says as we make our way to the platform, our luggage bumping along the concrete path behind us.

After a quick ride, we arrive at the busy central station in Rome. Ed looks at the departure postings and checks our tickets.

"Our train to Naples is delayed. We've got a two-hour layover," he announces.

In my normal life, two hours wouldn't be a big deal, but this is my sleep-deprived, jet-lagged, 'I brushed my teeth in a public bathroom and have slept in my clothes' self. I don't have two hours of patience left and I can tell the others feel the same way. We find seats in one of the station's cafes and grab a snack, but this is no place to linger. As soon as we've eaten our last bites, the server swoops in to wipe off our table in preparation for the next batch of layover travelers.

We wander back to the terminal, pulling our luggage through the crowds. A group of young people dressed in Comic-Con outfits—superheroes and villains with orange hair, capes and tights— laugh as they dart in front of us. At least someone is having fun. Finding no available seats, we plop down on the floor with our luggage and wait. I put my head on my suitcase and close my eyes.

Now I'm thinking we should have booked one of those packaged tours where you get on a bus and they plan everything for you. Someone moves your luggage from place to place and you likely don't end up on the floor in the Roma Central train terminal using your carry-on as a pillow. I remind myself that this is all part of the adventure, yet I'm relieved when our train arrives.

We stow our bags in the bins above our first-class accommodations and settle in. Ed and I face Anne and Scott with a table between us, boy-girl, boy-girl, like the train scene from the movie *White Christmas*, but instead of Vermont, we are on our way to Naples. Morale soars as the attendant arrives.

"What can I get for you?" he asks. "We have water, soft drinks, beer, wine, Prosecco, snacks..."

Anne grins and orders a Prosecco, Ed orders red wine, and Scott asks for a Coke Zero.

"And for you?" the steward asks me.

"I'll have a Coke Zero as well," I say, thinking it's a little early in the day to start drinking.

"Oh Madame," he shakes his head. "Why would you order that when you can have a Prosecco?"

Indeed. Welcome to Italy where any hour is happy hour. I stick with my original order, but down a generous portion of Anne's Prosecco when she offers me a sip. After a pleasant ride, we arrive at the station in Naples and find our pre-arranged driver waiting for us. With a brief introduction, he takes my oversized tote bag, slides it over the handle of my roller bag, and darts off.

"I need the bathroom," I whisper to Ed as we dash through the crowd.

"Why didn't you go on the train?" he grumbles. "I didn't need to go then, but I had that Coke and half of Anne's Prosecco. I don't think I can make it all the way to Sorrento. Doesn't anyone else need to go?"

No one does. I hurry to catch up to the driver. "Bathroom? Toilet?" I ask.

He stops, annoyed. "Bathroom, yes, this way." We follow as he drags my luggage down a flight of stairs.

"This won't take long," I say, but stop short at the turnstile at the bathroom entrance. This is not a free-pee. Rummaging through my purse, I find a half-eaten roll of TUMs, lip gloss, a bottle of hand sanitizer, my phone, and sunglasses.

"Anyone have a euro coin?" I ask my traveling companions.

"Use your card," the driver snaps.

Reluctantly, I put my credit card into the machine and the door swings open. I can't believe I have to charge one euro to my account. What will the description on the bank statement say? City of Naples Sanitation Department? The Toilet Mafia? Here She Goes Again? If I continue this trend, the bank will track me throughout this trip via my pit stops. I make a mental note: carry change for potty money.

Upon exiting the train station, I see why our driver is impatient. It's rush hour in Naples and he's parked (illegally?) at the side of a busy road. He throws our luggage into the back of the van, ushers us into our seats, and zooms into traffic to the sound of honking and shouting. He drives with one hand on the wheel, brandishing his other out the window at his fellow drivers.

"Where are you from?" he asks.

We attempt light conversation, but are distracted by the crazy drivers. I hold my breath as we approach a traffic circle unlike anything I've ever seen. There are at least four lanes of traffic, maybe more, but in actuality, there are no lane markings. We are in the middle of a pack of cars jockeying for position as they attempt to enter or exit the circle from all sides. I'm reminded of a catastrophic demolition derby my dad once took me to when I was a child. I squeeze my eyes shut and brace myself for the sound of squealing tires and crunching metal, but miraculously, we emerge unscathed and soon leave the city behind us.

When we told our travel agent we wanted to see Naples, she suggested we stay in Sorrento instead. Now I understand why. My first impression of Naples is a busy, gritty city, not the storybook Italian village that tourists imagine. Yet, I am a little sad while glancing through the rearview mirror. Maybe we didn't give it a fair chance. After all, the city that invented pizza can't be all bad.

"How long will it take to get to Sorrento?" Ed asks our driver.

"Some days, twenty minutes," he says, "on other days, ninety."

This is a ninety-minute day. I rest my head against the window, close my eyes, and doze until Anne nudges me.

"I think that's Mt. Vesuvius!" she says.

From the car, it looks unassuming. Not much more than a large hill and not at all what I was expecting from the volcano that destroyed Pompeii several times over, but the driver nods his head to confirm. Anne snaps a few photos to send to her science department friends.

The scenery changes as we enter the town of Sorrento. Small shops and houses line the narrow roads that twirl around this coastal town like linguine. As we approach the city center, the shops and restaurants take on a more sophisticated vibe, catering to tourists and Italians on holiday. The traffic is moving at a steady pace. Scooters dart in and out among the cars, but drivers are amicable and our driver's mood lightens. We pull up to the Hotel Michelangelo behind a large bus blocking the entrance. Two men unload a mountain of luggage from its underbelly.

The Tour Bus Travelers have beaten us here. They are probably refreshed and enjoying drinks around the pool by now. I drag my own bags to the front desk—the luggage that traveled from Tucson to Atlanta to Rome to Naples to Sorrento in the past day and a half. The luggage I will heave into vans and onto busses, planes, and boats before this trip is over. I'm exhausted, but I feel a sense of satisfaction. We're in Italy!

# Good Morning, Italy
## Buongiorno, Italia

I fumble in the dark and squint at my phone. 2
am. I've traveled over six thousand miles in twenty-
four hours, yet my body remains on Tucson time. I
close my eyes and try to go back to sleep. *It's night in
Sorrento... see, Ed is sleeping.* I stare at the ceiling.
Maybe some yoga relaxation will help. *Breathe in...
breathe out... breathe in...*

Nope, still awake. I slip out of bed, feel my way
to the bathroom, and back into position. As my
backside lightly touches down, I'm surprised by the
cold, porcelain rim and, at first, I think Ed has left
the seat up. But no, it's... I jump up and flip on the
lights. The bidet glares at me. *Sorry, so sorry.* I
mumble as I move to the toilet, noting for future
reference, that it is the second fixture from the door.

In the morning, I tell Ed about my nighttime
adventure.

"That's hilarious!" he says.

"It was disgusting!" I gripe, but then the scene
replays in my mind.

He's right. It is funny. However, I decide not to
share this with Anne and Scott when we meet for

breakfast. We travel close, but practice decorum when it comes to bathroom talk. This would fall under our unwritten travel taboo—too much information. After the maître d' shows us to our seats, he invites us to the buffet.

The morning buffet is truly a work of art. Platters of sliced prosciutto, assorted cheeses and loaves of crusty bread load the tables, while sausages, scrambled eggs, bacon, and potatoes keep warm in buffet-style chafing dishes. Fresh fruit and pitchers of freshly squeezed blood-orange juice sparkle in the morning sun. For those who prefer lighter fare, there is an assortment of cereals and yogurts.

But who wants lighter fare when you can have pastries? Cornetti—large, flakey Italian croissants filled with cream, jam, or my favorite, chocolate—present themselves on gleaming serving trays. Elegant cake stands lift Italian tarts to celebrity status. Their fluted crusts are filled with frangipane (a creamy almond custard), jam, or chocolate. Sliced into slivers they are tiny bites to be savored, but I want to gobble them down and go back for more, eager to try each flavor.

Ed visits the coffee dispenser and returns with a large cup of espresso.

"Aren't you supposed to use one of those little cups for that?" I ask.

"Yeah, maybe."

He'll be wired up for the rest of the day. Italy is coffee country, and as a tea drinking enthusiast, I feel out of place. I ask a white-jacketed attendant for hot tea. He raises his eyebrows and disappears into the kitchen, returning with a teapot of boiling water, a cup and saucer, and a tea bag which he places at the table in front of me.

"You may help yourself, Madame," he informs me, pointing out the hot water and tea bags in an inconspicuous corner of the buffet.

When breakfast is over, I'm groggy from too little sleep and too much food, but I push on, excited about our first day in Italy. We have a full agenda. We walk a short distance to our meet-up spot and wait with other tourists lured by the promise of Limoncello (the area's trademark liqueur) and the opportunity to make our own wood-fired pizzas. As our group gathers, we chat with a young couple touring Italy and Greece.

"We want to try traveling together before committing to marriage," Sean says.

In his youthful naiveté, I think he has it backwards. The *true* test of a marriage is to live together for decades, *then* try traveling with each other. Sean's partner Dana is wearing an adorable short, flouncy sundress and I'm rethinking the outfit I'm wearing for this 'Lemon Farm Experience.' The black pull-on pants and Columbia hiking shirt were a practical choice, but now they seem matronly. When transportation arrives, we pile in a van with Sean and Dana, and a woman traveling with her daughter. Our driver navigates narrow, winding roads as we leave the coastal city of Sorrento and climb into the highlands. He points out entire lemon groves, covered in green netting, terraced along the hillsides. Now and then, I catch a glimpse of sapphire water as we climb and my heart races. The Mediterranean Sea.

During the planning phase, we listed our expectations for this trip. Visiting historical sites, enjoying good food and drink, and seeing beautiful scenery were all included. Yet, besides this, I have two specific wishes: to see Venice at sunrise, and to put my feet in the Mediterranean Sea. My first request will have to wait. Venice is the last stop on our itinerary, but I'm getting closer to being able to fulfill the second.

Why is walking in the Mediterranean so important to me? What do I hope to accomplish? I've been landlocked for a while now, stuck in mediocrity. Perhaps I'm seeking a baptism, a renewal, a freshness of spirit that is somehow tied to this ancient body of water. We will tour along the coast of Italy for the next few weeks. I just need to find the right opportunity.

But today, we seek lemons.

# How to Drink Limoncello
*Come Bere il Limoncello*

We round one last hairpin turn and enter the hamlet of Schiazzano. Bruno, lemon farmer, tour guide, and self-proclaimed mayor meets us at the village store, a tiny building that serves as the town center, restaurant, and gathering place. Bruno is an ample, gregarious man, with a booming voice and ready smile. After greeting us in perfect English, we are invited into the local cathedral to begin the tour.

As I step through the humble facade, this small, 14th century church dedicated to the Blessed Savior reveals its glory. I look up and gasp. Soaring three stories high, the vaulted ceiling is white and airy and tinged with gold as if angels are swirling about, outlining the clouds with glitter.

I walk towards the altar, my footsteps echoing on tiles worn from centuries of weddings, funerals, and baptisms, yet well cared for as this sacred place continues to function as the heart of the village. Two rows of humble, wooden pews line a central aisle leading to the elaborate altar. I stop to examine an intricate design on the floor. A golden star shape with azure points extends the length of the aisle and under the pews. It looks familiar, yet unexpected, on the floor of a cathedral. I can't quite figure it out. Bruno soon answers my question.

"It's a compass rose," he announces to the group, "a tribute to the sailors who funded the church's renovations in the 16th century. And in the tile mosaics, you will find images of grapes but no lemons. Why? Lemons are not native to this area. Sailors brought them over from India and China and cultivated them as a source of revenue."

Our guide pauses and his words resonate through the cathedral as the floor tells the story. After giving us several moments to explore, the tour moves on.

"Now, let us see what we have done with these transplants the sailors brought us," Bruno smiles and waves us towards the door, eager to show off his lemon farm.

As our group shuffles out of the building, I stay behind fascinated with the design on the floor. Ah, yes, a compass rose. I see it now. Its longest arm points towards the altar and to the sea beyond. I stand in its center, with my arms outstretched, and gaze at the infinite possibilities of directions spread out before me.

"Deb?" Ed pokes his head into the church and motions for me, jarring me back to reality. I leave my thoughts behind, and hurry to catch up with the group.

Up ahead, Bruno walks us through the village on a series of meandering lanes, impossible for most cars to navigate.

"These were donkey paths," he informs us, "and at one time, the only way to get in or out of town."

As we walk, he greets his neighbors.

"Everybody knows everybody here. The same three families have lived in this village for generations and own most of the groves."

I glance through a gate into a courtyard. Two women sit on the steps watching a child race around on a plastic scooter. I wonder how they managed to get their car through the town and into the courtyard.

We walk through an ancient tunnel and I imagine donkeys walking along, their hooves clacking on the worn stone path. The tunnel opens into another courtyard that I suspect is Bruno's back yard. He waves to a toddler peeking through the window of a modest home. We gather and our guide prepares us:

"So now, we come to the lemons. You will see green netting supported by stakes covering the entire grove."

"Does it keep out the mosquitos?" asks a woman as she swats one away.

"Ah, unfortunately no. The netting is there to help keep the temperature of the grove constant and increase the growing season. It protects the lemons from the blistering summer sun and the winter freeze. Now we can see up-close. Come." He motions for us to follow and we duck under the canopy of netting to enter the cool, shady grove.

I think there must be some mistake. Instead of an industrial lemon-producing operation, it's an enchanted fairy garden. The dirt path is soft under my feet and the aroma of warm, moist earth and lemons surrounds me. We wander around the hillside and pass a small glass-paned garden shed borrowed from one of Beatrice Potter's children's books. I almost expect to see Peter Rabbit underneath a terra-cotta pot. Lemon trees in various stages of growth are everywhere, yet in among them I see olive trees, a few grape vines, and yes, even a zucchini plant or two. No space is wasted.

"Now I will let you in on a little secret. Look." Bruno points to the trunk of a sapling. "This part, the root and the trunk up to here, this is an orange tree. We graft the lemon trees onto the orange tree. This makes lemon trees stronger, more able to resist disease. One supports another to strengthen it."

A young man who has been assisting our guide picks a lemon from a mature tree.

"These are certified Sorrento Lemons only grown in this region of Italy," he says as he slices the fruit. The juice runs down his hand and he pares the lemon into small bits he offers for tasting. The fruit is sweet and tart all at once.

"Good, yes?" he continues. "But here... it's the peel that is our fortune. Sorrento lemons are famous for it. Scratch it with your fingernail. See the oil? Ahhhh... now we have the makings of Limoncello!"

His remark elicits a cheer from the group and we make our way out of the lemon grove.

"Hey guys, stop!" I say. "I want a picture of the four of us."

I am a writer, often stopping to take a photo or write a word or phrase on my phone, the raw material I will use to create albums, blog posts, and stories. Used to this, my husband and friends are usually patient with me, yet now they are anxious to move on. I only get one shot and the picture is goofy, but I love the real-life moment it captures. The packable (but dorky) sunhat I thought I needed is smashed down on my head. Scott is barely in the photo at all. You can just see a corner of his face and his eyes are looking off to the right to see where the tour group has gone. Anne smiles over Scott's head, and tall Ed is in the background. He's standing behind a branch and it looks like his head is grafted onto it like a human lemon tree. We rejoin the tour and walk back to the village store.

"Now we take my Ferrari to the limoncello tasting!" Bruno gestures towards a bright red golf cart. "See!" he laughs and points to the Ferrari sticker he's attached to the side of the vehicle. Two other golf carts join the entourage to transport us in groups of three or four to the next stop on our tour.

When it's our turn, Scott gets up front with the driver—Ed, Anne, and I squeeze into the back—and we begin our roller coaster ride along the donkey paths. Our driver seems to delight in scaring us as he zooms up and over hills. He taps twice on the toy-car horn at each hairpin turn "just in case someone is coming around the corner," he says, making no attempt to slow down.

We arrive at the farmhouse, where they have set up an outdoor kitchen and a tasting table. The air smells of sea and salt and...something else.

"It's a farm, Deb. You're smelling hay and cows and manure," Scott says. He knows his... stuff. He and Anne have a small farm in Southern Indiana.

"I was expecting lemons," I say.

The farm is a family business. Bruno's sister offers glasses of local red and white wine while the barn cats walk among us, rubbing up against selected legs. Anne and I take our wine and sit on a low stone wall to watch the boats sail along the bay of Naples. The Mediterranean sun kisses my face as I gaze at the blue-green water.

When called to the tasting tables, we sample fresh-squeezed olive oil infused with local herbs and spices. We dip small squares of bread into the oil and experience the flavors of Italy–basil, rosemary, oregano, lemon. From there, we take our seats around the outdoor kitchen and prepare for a cooking demonstration.

"You come for limoncello, yes? But this is a farm, and I want to show you what else we offer here," Bruno dons his apron and continues. "So, we have cows and from these cows we get milk, and from this milk we make cheese." He picks up a pitcher and pours the creamy, white liquid into a large metal bowl which he sets on a hot plate. "At just the right temperature, the milk separates into curds and whey."

Curds and whey? The stuff Little Miss Muffett ate when she sat on her tuffet? This gets my attention. After years of teaching nursery rhymes to kindergarteners, I never understood what was in her bowl. If Miss Muffett had been Italian, she would have been making cheese.

Bruno sets the whey aside and manipulates the curds into a large lump. Then, with a few flicks of his wrist, he transforms the lump into a beautiful braid.

"Mozzarella!"

He raises his masterpiece over his head with both hands, enjoying oohs and aahs from the crowd, then cuts off pieces of the freshly-made cheese. His two young nephews pass around samples. The farm cats know the routine. They weave around our feet, hoping for a treat, but they don't find any under my chair. The fresh mozzarella melts in my mouth and I leave nothing on my paper plate.

"Good, huh?" Bruno smiles. He knows his work is impressive, but there is more to come.

"Here, we leave nothing to waste. Now we make ricotta—*cotta* meaning cooked, *ri* meaning twice or again. So, *ricotta* is twice cooked."

He takes the whey and reheats it, and soon we sample the creamy-smooth cheese that lasagna dreams are made of. Now I know I'm in love, not only with the food, but the music of the language. When Bruno says 'ri-cot-ta' it's not *staccato*, the way I say it, but he blends the sounds slowly, up and down like a melody in *legato* lingering on the last note: *reee-KAAAH- taaahhh.*

There is one more treat, compliments of the cows and Bruno's sister. *Panna Cotta* (cooked cream) is a mixture of sweetened cream, vanilla, and gelatin, set in molds and refrigerated. The sister brings it out and her young sons scurry to serve each guest. I scrape my bowl clean, I think, but when I set it on the ground, a gray and white striped kitten finishes what my spoon missed. The dessert is popular with tourists and felines alike.

"We are done now, OK?" Bruno plays with us. "Ok, Ok... I know what you want. You come for the limoncello. I will tell you this, but you must tell no one. You can make limoncello for yourself. Only three things: lemon peel, sugar, vodka. That's all," he holds up three fingers one at a time to make his point. "Before you buy it at the store, check the label. If it has more than these three things, you waste your money. If they do not make it with Sorrento lemons, you waste your money." He grins.

After receiving a small cup, I take a sip of the sweet/tart liquid and am transported back to the lemon grove. Limoncello is a digestif liqueur, meant to be savored slowly after a meal. A second seductive sip leaves me to believe it could be dangerously addictive.

At this point, the tour takes an interesting twist and becomes a combination game show and college kegger. "Who likes limoncello?" our golf-cart driver asks. Everyone raises their hands.

"You." He says, pointing to a young man in our group. "Come on up. What is your name?"

"Brian."

"Brian, you say you like limoncello?"

"Yes," Brian answers.

"OK, tip your head back."

"Let's cheer him on..."

The group gets into the act and we clap and shout in unison:

"*Brian... Brian... Brian.*"

Brian tips back his head and our driver pours a stream of the yellow liquid directly from the bottle into Brian's mouth. He swallows, gives a thumbs up and returns to his seat. The group cheers and the host chooses another volunteer. This time it's Dana, in the cute sundress. She leans back in the chair and I am relieved that her dress covers... enough. She laughs and tosses her head back and the young man pours limoncello into her mouth while we clap and chant:

"*Dana, Dana, Dana.*"

I think perhaps this drinking game is something I missed as a young woman. Ed and I married while we were in college and had kids a few years after we graduated. I became 'responsible adult' quickly.

When asked if anyone else wants to try, I look at Ed, Scott, and Anne and *almost* volunteer. But I don't. I hold back for fear of...of what? Looking ridiculous? Embarrassing myself? Death by limoncello? Why can't I be more like Dana? I came to Italy for a transformation. I had a chance to burst out of the Bubble and I blew it. The game is over. Our host fills our limoncello glasses again for a final toast.

"*Salute!*"

I halfheartedly raise my glass with the others. Then...

*It's not too late,* Italy whispers. *Do it your way.*

Silently cheering myself on, I tip back my head, bring the cup to my lips, and let the golden liquid slip down my throat. A warm smile crosses my face.

As we prepare to leave the lemon farm, I think back to where I started the tour, standing in the center of the cathedral's compass rose as I pondered the possibilities before me. Now I think I understand. This journey doesn't require me to become a different person, but I will have opportunities to explore, taste, observe, laugh, and grow. I need only to take the first step. Italy is speaking to me. It may take some time, but I'm learning its language.

Bruno's marketing strategy works. Our last taste of limoncello convinces the group that we must have more. We all buy bottles to take home. Our foursome is one of the last to leave and we ride with the same driver we had before. This time, Anne jumps into the front seat of the golf cart.

"No seatbelts," the cute driver says. "Put your arm over here and hold on."

Anne scoots closer and throws her arm across the back of the seat behind the driver's shoulders. I snap a picture as she looks back at me and flashes a girlish grin. In the photo, it looks like she has her arm around him.

"Limoncello..." I mouth.

It's pure gold.

# Pizza Love
## *Pizza Amore*

Along with the lemon farm and the cathedral, the village of Schiazzano has one other attraction. We descend ancient stone steps and duck through the arched doorway of the town's pizzeria where we hope to make our own pizzas. There is no signage on the door, but it makes no difference. Locals know where to come, and even if you are new to the city, the aroma of fresh baked bread and rich tomato sauce coming from the wood stove would lead you here. They have modernized the interior of the centuries-old building, yet it maintains its vintage style. Red and white checkered cloths and vases of fresh flowers adorn round tables where a few people are enjoying a late lunch. A woman at the hostess stand stops folding boxes for takeout orders.

"This way," she says leading us into a tiny kitchen.

The monumental wood-fired stove burnished charcoal-black from decades of use, takes center stage. Its iconic curved opening glows with crimson coals like the gates of Hell or a one-eyed dragon spewing waves of heat into the room. A fan twirling in the window above the industrial sink is working overtime. Behind a stainless-steel table stands a small man with graying hair, a trim mustache and wire-rimmed glasses. He wears jeans, a white tee shirt and a clean white apron tied around his waist. A young woman is at his side.

"Ciao! Welcome! My name is Sophia," she says. "My uncle Franco and I are your chefs and teachers in this pizzeria that has been in our family for three generations. It is our pizza, but also our passion that we will share with you today."

Franco nods and smiles, content to let his niece do the talking. Because of cramped conditions, we will work in pairs. It's hard for Ed and I to wait, but soon it's our turn. Franco takes a ball of dough that has been rising in a covered container. His experienced hands move quickly, flattening and stretching the dough into a dinner-plate sized circle.

"Now for the moment you've been waiting for!" Sophia says.

On cue, Franco tosses the circle of dough high in the air, letting it spin and stretch, then catches it at exactly the right moment. We laugh and clap in amazement as he repeats the process with the next ball, then places the perfect circles of dough in front of us. I see now that this is more of a *demonstration* than the *class* we had expected, but no matter. It is so much fun to watch the master at work. However, so as not to leave us totally out of the process,

Franco invites us to assemble the pizza. Under his watchful eye, I ladle a generous amount of sauce onto the dough and use the back of the utensil to spread the liquid, tomato-y goodness almost to the edge.

"We make the sauce here. Local tomatoes, garlic, basil. Simple. Now we add some of Bruno's freshly made mozzarella." Sophia hands each of us a section of creamy white cheese and instructs us to pinch off small bits to distribute around the sauce. "And we bake."

Franco ceremoniously takes a large wooden paddle from a hook on the wall. In a series of smooth movements, he shoves the paddle under my tomato and mozzarella topped circle of dough and slides it off onto the glowing stone floor of the oven. Immediately the crust puffs, and the mozzarella bubbles over the tomato sauce releasing a burst of aroma that lights up every appetite neuron in my brain. While the pizza bakes, Sophia explains we are making Pizza Margherita, in the traditional Neapolitan style.

"According to the legend, Pizza Margherita was invented near here in the 1800s to honor Queen Margherita of Savoy and the unification of Italy. See the colors of the Italian flag? Red tomatoes, white mozzarella, and here is the green," Sophia says breaking off a stem of fresh basil for each of us.

The pizzas bake quickly and Franco knows exactly the right moment to pull them out–when the crust is golden brown with a few bits of char from the intense heat and heavenly blobs of mozzarella have melted over the sauce. He slides each one onto an oversized dinner-plate. It can barely hold the twelve-inch pizza, more than enough to serve two people, but we each get our own. In a final flourish, we tear basil leaves and toss them onto our creations.

"No sharing allowed," Sophia says.

And it's a good thing because I don't want to share. Ed and I carry our masterpieces to the table and join Anne and Scott, already enjoying theirs. I'm not one of those people who take pictures of their food, but this pizza is beautiful. I pick up one wedge and take my first bite. It's pizza love. The crust is perfect–crispy yet light and puffy–the result of its brief yet intense time in the wood-fired oven. The combination of tomato, basil, and olive oil is heavenly. When I bite into the mozzarella, it strings down my chin. Extra napkins all around.

If you come to Italy expecting the American stuffed crust-extra cheese-sausage-pepperoni-the works concoction that late night takeout orders are made of, this simple pie might disappoint you. But if you approach this pizza with an open mind, you will experience pure Italy–simple, fresh, authentic.

Amore.

# My Name Is
## *Mi Chiamo*

Today, we are visiting the ancient ruins of Pompeii—a destination at the top of our list of must-sees for this trip. I remember reading about Pompeii in school, many, many years ago. Textbook images of people in togas running ahead of a stream of red-hot lava come to my mind in cartoonish fashion, yet I'll admit to not understanding the events that led to the city's destruction in 79 AD or what to expect when we get to the site. So, we travel.

Our driver meets us in front of the hotel, and when he steps out of the van, I'm reminded of the movie *Men in Black*. Dressed in black, slim-fitting slacks, white shirt, dark tie, and sunglasses, he greets us briefly then opens the doors and we settle in—Ed in the front seat, Anne, Scott, and I in the back. The city of Sorrento is awake. Its residents zoom to work via scooters or tiny cars, dodging tour buses and vans transporting tourists to their destinations. Our driver moves effortlessly in and out of traffic.

"Where are you from?" he asks, the typical conversation starter.

"Arizona," Ed gestures towards me.

"Arizona. Cactus." The young man grins.

"And we live in Indiana," Scott points to himself and Anne.

"Indiana?" This stumps our driver.

"In the middle of the country. Farms.... Indy 500."

"Ah, yes! Race cars!"

We've made our first connection.

"I am sorry. My English is... not so good. In school I did not learn it, but now I learn from my passengers when I am driving." He glances in the rearview mirror and smiles.

"What is your name?" I say. A look of concern crosses our driver's face. "Francesco. Here." He holds up his photo ID. Perhaps he thinks we are looking for proof that he is a verified English-speaking driver. Or maybe he's not concerned, but surprised that we have taken an interest in him.

"Everything's fine," I reassure him.

Thinking this would be an excellent opportunity to practice Italian, the language I'm falling in love with, I take out my phone and set my translation app. I type 'my name is.'

"*Mi chiamo, Deb*," I say, hoping the pronunciation is correct.

"Deb," Francesco beams at me in the rearview mirror, encouraging me to continue.

"*Mi chiamo Ed*," I point to my husband.

44

"No, no. *Suo* *chiamo* *Ed.*" We both laugh. I correct my mistake and continue with introductions.

"Now we are learning from you!" I remark.

As we leave the city and move along the coast towards Naples and Pompeii, Francisco gets a call and I listen as he speaks in rapid Italian. I close my eyes and let the words flow over me. They float up and down with an abundance of vowels and soft *ch* *and sh* sounds, making this mundane conversation lyrical. The scenery fluctuates as we approach Naples. Now a strip of countryside full of small stone homes complete with humble gardens, laundry flapping from clotheslines, and assorted vehicles parked about; now a breathtaking view of the sea. Anne turns to our driver.

"Do you have a family?"

"*Si*. My wife, Mia, and a son and daughter. Cloe is eleven months and Salvadore, he is four years." With one eye on the road, he taps his phone and flashes their pictures towards us. "Salvadore, he is very... active. He will start school in two weeks."

"We were teachers," I say, then use my translator app. "*Insegnanti*"

Francesco pauses, "Oh, *professori*," he says. "For what age?"

"Three of us in high school. Big kids..." Scott holds his hand above his head. "...and Deb taught little kids, like Salvadore."

"Aye, yi, yi. So sorry for you!" our driver laughs and slaps his forehead. "You are not working now? You are on holiday?" he asks.

"Retired, *pensionato*." I say.

"We're old." Ed chimes in with a grin.

"No, no. You are not old." Francesco counters, perhaps to flatter us, yet when Anne tells him how old we are, he raises his eyebrows.

"In Italy, is very different," he says. "People at your age are very old. They sit at home, not active like you."

My friends and I smile. With Francesco's words, the years fall away and the jet lag and minor aches and pains we had been grumbling about at breakfast vanish. We are young and adventurous.

"Have you been a driver for a long time?" Ed asks.

"Yes," Francesco pauses, "but during the pandemic, everything in Italy shut down. No tourists. There were not jobs for drivers."

"That must have been really hard." Anne says.

Francesco gets quiet.

We had visited Italy the first time in the fall of 2019. Six months later, the country dissolved into chaos as the first few COVID cases rapidly multiplied. Italy was the first country to implement a national quarantine, and we were shocked to see images on the news of overcrowded hospitals, bodies piling up in makeshift morgues, and daily death toll reports. Little did we know we would soon see similar scenes in our own country.

"Yes, it was hard," Francesco continues. "My wife and kids and I moved in with my parents. We stayed home and took care of each other, then I took a job as an ambulance driver."

I picture Francesco spending his days and nights driving sick and dying people to the hospital at a risk to himself and his young family.

"How did you stay safe?" I ask.

"I wore special clothing from here to here and a big, big mask." Francesco makes a motion from his head to his feet, then remains silent for several moments. "But you know, Italy, it is strong. We have overcome much and the people come together and now, we go on. Now tourists are back. The drivers work again." He smiles. "This is better."

We see exit signs for Pompeii. Mt. Vesuvius is in sight and the closer we get, the more impressive it becomes. This is the purpose of our journey today, yet this drive, this interaction with Francesco is priceless. We came to see the sights, but it is the people we meet who will make Italy come alive. Francesco pulls into the visitor parking lot and opens the doors for us. Before we leave, I use my translator once again. I want Francisco to know I appreciate him learning my language and I am honored to attempt his. I type:

You are a good driver. Thank you.

*Sei un buon pilota. Grazie.*

I show Francesco my phone and we say the words together, first in English, then in Italian. He places his hand over his heart and nods his head at each of us.

*"Grazie, grazie."*

# A Day in Pompeii
## *Una Giornata a Pompei*

All tour guides should have these eyes. Aquamarine. Exactly the color of the sea. I want to walk around the ruins at Pompeii with this man all day, and perhaps bring him home as a souvenir. Mattia speaks perfect English... with an Italian flair. I can say the same for his appearance. He is remarkably tall, sporting khaki shorts, a white linen shirt—untucked with the sleeves rolled up—and trendy athletic shoes (no socks). He has pulled his dark, longish hair back in a man-bun, and he is sporting just the right amount of stubble. Sunglasses hang casually from the place where he had stopped unbuttoning his shirt. Anne and I exchange a sideways glance.

"We will start here," Mattia says pointing to a large map on the visitor center wall. "Pompeii is an active archaeological site. Only one-third of it is currently excavated and archeologists are making new discoveries each day. They find that many other civilizations are buried beneath Pompeii, layer upon layer. It is fascinating. Sorry, but I get so passionate each time I come here. See I have goosebumps."

Mattia thrusts his forearm towards us. He is close enough for me to see the tiny bumps forming on his tanned skin. The bumps are contagious.

"I'll get our tickets and meet you back here. Now is a good time to get a bottle of water or an espresso if you like," he says as he walks away.

"This is going to be intense," I whisper to Anne.

"You mean the tour or the guide?"

"Yeah," I sigh and we giggle.

Large tour groups swarm around us, following their flag-carrying leaders like sheep towards the entrance. Mattia returns with our tickets and I am glad, in more ways than one, that our travel agent has arranged a private tour guide for us. He waves our passes to the attendant and we slip through the gate, then stop at the wall surrounding the ancient city.

"Before we enter the museum. I must prepare you. You will see many artifacts, but also, the evidence of death. Sometimes, you might feel overwhelmed, but it is part of the story. What you will see are not actual bodies, but casts made of the people who died when Vesuvius erupted. I want to show you how they made the casts of the bodies."

We gather around Mattia's phone where he has downloaded a video of the casting process. I learn the people did not die in a lava flow, as I was picturing. Experts believe that those left behind died instantaneously, overcome by toxic fumes and extreme heat. As a blanket of ash covered the dead, it hardened into pumice that initially preserved the bodies. Over time, their flesh decomposed leaving a perfect mold formed in the rock. In 1860 a man named Giuseppe Fiorelli developed a way to inject plaster into the molds. Archeologists then painstakingly removed the pumice to reveal the human forms in remarkable detail.

As we enter the museum, we see evidence of the civilizations that once thrived. Exquisite pottery and decorative scenes painted on walls are miraculously preserved, evidence of extravagant lifestyles. Mattia stops and points to an object in a display case.

"What do you think this is?" he asks.

"A bowl?" I reply.

"No, a colander," Anne says. "See the perforations."

"Ah, yes, a simple kitchen utensil, but look at the elaborate detail. The people of Pompeii valued artistic expression."

We pass many more cases of preserved pottery and other artifacts. Then Mattia stops before entering the next exhibit.

"And now the casts." He lowers his voice.

I think I'm prepared, yet as we enter the room containing the cast bodies, I realize I'm not.

Tourists who had been chatting or laughing fall silent. The video prepared me for the scientific and factual information, but not the raw emotion I feel as I see the figures before me. The gray casts reveal eerie details of people experiencing the moment of death. It is a room full of agony. I see a figure, face down, and I can imagine a person trying to flee but falling as fumes overcame him. Another, with a round belly appears seated or reclining. Perhaps he was a wealthy man reluctant to abandon his home and wealth. At what point did he realize he had waited too long to escape?

And for me, the most heart-wrenching figure of all, a mother holding an infant. Did she snatch the baby up at the last moment to shield it with her own body? Did she plead to the gods with her last breath? Near the mother, a perfectly detailed child, its mouth open, and I can almost hear echoes of the toddler's cries as he or she fell to the ground. In each case, the hands clench and arms draw in towards the bodies. I mention this to Mattia.

"Yes, the hands are disturbing to me as well. It is thought to be an involuntary cadaver spasm, a result of the sudden heat shock on the corpse."

The air in the museum is too warm and the walls are closing in on me. I take a few pictures, then stop; it seems wrong to be capturing these images. Leaving the corpse room I walk through the rest of the exhibit quickly, relieved at last when we reach the outside air. Mattia leads us away from the museum. He too, seems glad to have escaped for now.

"OK, so now we will see the remains of the city. Because ash covered it so quickly, this site is a well-preserved picture of a Roman city."

Mattia leads us to the Forum of Pompeii, the center of the once thriving metropolis. At the far end of the Forum, Mt. Vesuvius dominates the landscape. Still an active volcano, it is regarded as one of the most dangerous volcanoes in the world because of the millions of people living near enough to be affected by an eruption. The main street of the city is paved with large stepping stones that would have kept Roman feet dry from rainwater and waste. Remains of homes, businesses and public bathhouses give clues to daily lives of a people who were oblivious to the looming disaster and ill-equipped to escape. Intricate tile work on well-preserved floors depicts scenes of the day or detailed geometric works. Scott stops to examine an elaborate design. Done in black and white miniscule tiles, it depicts two athletes poised to spar in a wrestling match.

"Look at this," he says. "The sign says it was the entrance to a gymnasium and health spa. Amazing."

We walk around the ruins of the theater, the site of community and sporting events, where stone amphitheater seats remain in astounding condition.

Then Mattia leads us through the somber quarters underneath, where they kept slaves and tournament animals.

"Mt. Vesuvius gave some warning signs—we have written records of rumblings, landslides, and gas emissions. Most Pompeiians had time to leave, and many did, or tried to. They have found the skeletons of hundreds who fled to the seaside city of Herculaneum and gathered in the vaulted boat sheds as they waited to be evacuated, only to die instantly from the intense heat of the eruption. But many stayed too late and died here in Pompeii. Why? Maybe they ignored the warnings. Some were slaves or poor and had no means to leave. Some of the wealthy refused to leave and died clutching their treasures."

I thought of the panic and desperation the people must have felt in those last days of Pompeii. I have never lived in the shadow of a volcano, yet I live in the desert Southwest where evacuations from wildfires are becoming increasingly common. During the summer of 2020, the Bighorn Fire started from a lightning bolt that struck the Catalina Mountains just a few miles from my Arizona home. At night Ed and I could see the angry orange flames from our backyard. Our home was not in the fire's path, and fortunately, there were no lives or homes lost in the Bighorn fire. But what if I had to evacuate my home suddenly? What could I leave behind knowing I would never see it again? What would I hold on to?

Mattia glances at his watch and I sense our tour is nearing the end.

"Ah, the time. I never have enough time to tell everything. Your driver will be upset with me."

We hurry back to the visitor's center, thank our guide, and say goodbye. I look once more into those eyes, and then he's gone, off to lead another group. Perhaps another American tourist will fall in love.

On the ride back to our hotel, I lose interest in the scenery between Naples and Sorrento and spend my time on my phone scrolling through the pictures I've taken on our trip so far:

*'Here we are eating a delightful meal at an outdoor cafe overlooking the Mediterranean Sea; here we are at the lemon grove sipping limoncello; here are some dead people...'*

I stare at the images of the few corpse casts I've captured at Pompeii. My fingers clench, then I shove the phone back into the secure compartment in my purse and latch the zipper. No, I will not be posting these. Mattia's words haunt me:

*Some died.*

*Clutching their treasures.*

# Dressed
## *Vestito*

Ed and Scott notice her first. They turn their heads in unison, like a pair of synchronized swimmers as they walk down the busy Sorrento sidewalk on the way to dinner. Anne and I follow their gaze in time to see the young, stiletto-shod woman click across the street. Her white blouse sweeps low, revealing bronzed shoulders, and her long, dark hair bounces as she approaches the baby blue Vespa.

"Those heels are at least four inches," Scott affirms. He considers himself an expert on the subject, having put himself through college working part time in a shoe store.

"I don't see how she walks in them," Ed says.

The shoes are only part of the attraction, however. Our husbands slow down, waiting to see how the beautiful young woman will get astride her scooter. She bends over to place her purse into the saddlebag, and I am relieved to see that what looks like a mini-skirt is actually a pair of flowy short-shorts. At least she's covered her assets—just barely. She tosses her hair, puts on a pair of oversized sunglasses, and straps on her helmet. An older Italian man leaning against a doorway takes a last drag on his cigarette and drops it on the sidewalk. He extinguishes it with the toe of his shoe, then lets out a whistle, which the girl ignores as she speeds past. She makes it look so effortless—the shoes, the outfit, the hair, the sunglasses, the cute scooter.

That's what I was going for on our last trip to Italy when our foursome booked a Vespa tour at a vineyard outside of Florence. "Zoom around the Tuscan countryside on a Vespa," the online ad announced. I had no experience with scooters or motorcycles, and in fact, it had been several years since I'd ridden a bicycle, but the picture made it look so easy. When we arrived at the vineyard, they placed me in the 'novice' group and a guide gave me a quick lesson. This consisted of him running behind me shouting directions as my Vespa jerked and sputtered around the gravel parking lot.

"Get me off of this thing!" I screamed.

I didn't pass the driving test. None of us did, and we spent the afternoon drinking wine in the tasting room instead. Not a bad way to spend an afternoon by the way, but I was terribly disappointed. I had visions of driving around Italy on a Vespa, like Audrey Hepburn in the movie, *Roman Holiday*, or the real-life girl in the stilettos and short-shorts we'd just seen. Now I see where I went wrong. I wasn't dressed appropriately.

I've given up all hopes of driving around Italy on a scooter. Even so, there's something about that style, that attitude that I envy. I remember a remark my sister made when I was preparing for my first trip to Italy.

"Deb, you'll never be able to dress like an Italian woman. Just be yourself."

That's the problem. I don't want to be myself. Maybe I'd like to try on something different. In my former life as an elementary school teacher in the conservative Midwest, I conformed to a certain image, dictated by what would be professional, yet comfortable when I sat on tiny kindergarten chairs or on the floor. My go-to teacher outfit included an oversized, below-the-knee jumper with a season-themed turtleneck, tights, and sensible shoes. Sturdy, sensible, *ugly* shoes.

Oh, how I envy those stilettos!

After a nice dinner, we find an outdoor table at a gelateria along one of Sorrento's major streets. We are on a mission to find the best gelato in all of Italy and are prepared to do as much research as necessary. I'm tempted by the smorgasbord of attractively displayed flavors, yet when I go to the counter, I order the same thing I always order at the gelato shop back home—one scoop of salted caramel.

"That's what you always get. I thought we were going to try new things," Ed says.

"I know, but I really like salted caramel and I don't want to be disappointed with something different," I say.

I've always been an ice cream girl, but lately I've fallen in love with gelato. I like everything about it, even the tiny, plastic, shovel-shaped spoon that forces you to slow down, take tiny bites and savor the cool, creamy treat. They make ice cream and gelato from the same basic ingredients—cream, milk, and sugar, but gelato uses more sugar and less butterfat, making the flavors more intense. I was right. The salted caramel doesn't disappoint. From our sidewalk table vantage point, we watch a steady stream of people parading up and down the street.

"I can't believe how many people are here this late in the season. I thought if we waited until after Labor Day, the crowds would be down," Anne says.

"Our driver said that the city would be busy. This is the last week of vacation before the local schools start up again. Italians are on holiday." Scott reminds us.

A young woman in a white linen dress approaches and commands attention as her orange bikini shows through.

"The beach must be close," I say. "That girl is wearing her bathing suit under her dress."

"That's her underwear," Ed says.

"No, that has to be a swimsuit. No one would wear an orange bra and panties under a sheer dress," I say, but as she passes by, I suspect he's right.

We've been in Sorrento for several days now and I'm getting used to this sort of clothing from the younger crowd in this resort town. But as evening wears on, Sorrento comes alive with the *passeggiata,* a nightly ritual in which Italian families dress in finery and stroll around before dinner. The attire is timeless and classic. We notice women in well-fitted or flowy dresses in neutral colors accented with scarves or statement jewelry and exquisite leather shoes with matching handbags. There may be a hint of skin showing, but not too much. The 'embrace your gray hair' style that is now trending with mature American women (including Anne and I) is not catching on here. The Italian men we notice are classically dressed as well in linen shirts and slim-fitting slacks, and of course, quality leather footwear.

We finish our gelato and walk back towards the hotel in our own version of the *passeggiata.* Ed and Scott are ahead of us—Ed wearing his baggy-butt travel slacks, oversized Columbia shirt, and sneakers, and Scott sporting jeans, a polo, and cowboy boots.

"Our men are definitely not Italian," I whisper to Anne.

"What?" Ed says

"Nothing," we snicker.

"And we do not dress like Italian women," Anne says to me.

"I know, it's pretty obvious. What is it exactly that sets them apart?"

"Well, I'm not suggesting we get a mini-skirt or orange underwear, but there's something about the women our age. They're classic and confident."

"They embrace their femininity," I add.

It's dark now and the sidewalk cafes are bursting with fashionably dressed dinner crowds. Anne and I window shop, dropping further behind our husbands.

Suddenly, I stop. "Anne, we need to buy dresses!"

"I was thinking the same thing! Do you know how long it's been since I've worn a dress? Let's do it!"

We catch up to the guys and tell them we will meet at the rooftop bar at the hotel in an hour. With no time to lose, we duck inside the first women's clothing store we see. Heading to the sale rack, we dismiss the mini-dresses and strapless numbers and find a few styles that look promising. On a whim, I add a halter-type sundress to my collection and the sales clerk directs us to the dressing rooms.

I have high hopes for the sundress and slip the clingy, floral fabric over my head and down my torso, tying the halter straps around my neck. Instantly Italian. Yet, something isn't right. The built-in bra cups seem to have a mind of their own and aren't hitting me in the right places. I manipulate things around as best as I can. It's a trick I learned ages ago during my first bra experience.

Sooner or later, every young girl in my hometown ended up at Alden's ladies' shop for their first bra fitting. I was in the "later" category when my mother took me in for this rite of passage. I remember being embarrassed when the plump, gray-haired saleswoman approached.

"May I help you ladies?"

"We're here for her first bra," my mom announced in a much-too-loud-voice.

"Well, let's see what we can do," said the woman who would soon know me by my bra size. With an air of importance worthy of the measuring tape she wore around her neck, she ushered me into a fitting room.

After the mortifying measuring process, she returned with The Training Bra—a smaller, gentler version of a regular bra designed to train young women how to wear the contraptions of elastic and wire that will follow them throughout the rest of their lives.

"OK, let's see," the bra lady said as she fastened the last hook and eye.

As she looked me over, I could tell she wasn't satisfied.

"So, here's what you do, honey. Bend over and push your breasts up in there... There you go. See? Isn't that better?"

So that's what I'm doing decades later in an Italian dressing room when Anne calls out.

"Let me see when you get something on," she says from behind the curtain.

I give one last push, straighten the bodice, and step out of the changing room. Anne has on a black and white polka-dot dress that looks cute on her.

"Oh..." she says when she sees me. "Is the top *supposed* to fit like that? You look kind of... lopsided."

"Yeah, I'm not living up to its expectations. This dress is a no. I'll try the other one."

I return to the dressing room and put on a gray floral knit. It's better, but I'm not in love with it.

"I like that one!" Anne says when I model for her.

"I'm not sure. Why don't you try it on and I'll try the one you're wearing."

We return to our fitting rooms, slip off our dresses, and hand them through the curtains to make the exchange, giggling like two teenaged girls on our first trip to the mall without our moms. I'm not liking the dotted number on me either. It's just not my night, but the floral knit looks great on Anne and I tell her so.

"You need to buy that dress."

"But you saw it first. I can't take your dress," she says as she twirls in front of the mirror.

This is so typical of my sweet friend who often puts the needs and feelings of others before her own. I need to give her a little push.

"It looks better on you. Do it!"

It's the truth. The dress looks better on her than it did on me. Besides, how can I say no to the girl who hasn't worn a dress in decades?

"Then you won't have one. We're in this together. Try on that sundress on again," Anne says.

"Uh, no. When you add in the cost of the boob job, I will need in order to wear it, it's way out of my price range." We both laugh.

In the end, Anne buys the floral knit, and when she discovers all dresses are on end-of-summer clearance at sixty percent off, she buys the polka-dot one too. My friend loves a bargain.

"It's two to zero," she says as we hurry to meet the guys at the bar.

"What?"

"I have two dresses, you have zero. You need to catch up."

Game on.

# Traveling Lighter
## *Viaggiare Leggeri*

*"I've been one of those persons who never goes anywhere without a thermometer, a hot water bottle, a raincoat, and a parachute. If I had to do it again, I would travel lighter than I have."*
~ Nadine Stair

It's supposed to rain today, but I'm prepared. I take my travel-sized umbrella out of my suitcase and fasten it to the strap of my purse.

"You're not going to carry *that* around all day, are you?" Ed asks.

He'd said almost the same thing when he saw me pack it into my suitcase before we left Tucson.

"Yes. Yes, I am."

"You won't need it."

Ed hates to carry anything, especially when we travel. If it won't fit into a pocket, it stays behind. He likes to have a 'hands-free' experience. He's not the only one who feels this way. *"Don't waste valuable packing space on an umbrella, just pack a waterproof rain jacket,"* seasoned travelers often advise.

That's what I did when we were on our last trip to Italy. I left my umbrella at home. Though we had perfect weather for most of our trip, it poured on us the entire time we were on our walking tour of Rome and my *waterproof* jacket didn't live up to its name. What I remember most about the Coliseum was the way the rain dripped off my hood onto my nose and chin. I took shelter in the catacombs. While the guide was telling us the history of the Forum, I was trying to figure out why my jacket was absorbing water rather than repelling it. Savvy street vendors were selling cheap parasols at exorbitant prices, but Ed advised me not to buy one. So, I dripped. All day. Yes, this time, I'm taking my umbrella.

We tap on Anne and Scott's door to see if they are ready to leave for our Amalfi Coast experience.

"You're taking an umbrella?" Scott says when he sees me.

Sigh. The thing that no one thinks I need swings from my purse and bumps into my thigh with each step along the route to our meet-up place, where I noticed no one else is prepared for rain. Our optimistic travel companions are in shorts, tee shirts and yes, more sundresses.

One tourist stands out. Young, petite and blonde she's wearing a short, flouncy skirt with a matching top that exposes her tanned and toned midriff. It's fashioned out of a print that I'd seen in shop windows throughout Sorrento, a white and blue design embellished with large, yellow lemons. To top it off, she wears an enormous, woven sunhat with "CAPRI" written across the brim, advertising the popular island she must have recently visited. A matching oversized tote bag and glittery sandals complete the look. She's holding a large generic to-go cup that was probably filled with hotel coffee or more likely, she has found a local place to buy a designer latte. I bet she's missing her morning Starbucks; they are sparse in Italy. A large diamond ring flashes on her manicured left hand, and I imagine she and the attractive (also petite) man next to her are on their honeymoon. I name them The Capri Couple. An Instagram-worthy pair if ever I saw one, and I predict many beautiful posts in their future.

The tour group swells and spills out onto the parking lot as more people arrive.

"This doesn't look like the private tour, or even a small group tour we were expecting," Anne notices.

We check our tickets. We are in the right place, and after asking several people around us it looks like they are too. As departure time draws near, two young men distribute receivers and earbuds and show how to use them. We walk a short distance to where busses wait. The tour guides each take a group and we board one bus, our foursome taking the bench seat along the back. Our guide, Alessandro introduces himself. Though our minibus holds only about fifteen people, we'd hoped to avoid anything that felt like a bus tour. Nonetheless, we don our lanyards and earbuds and we're off.

Our hesitations vanish as we leave the city and wind along the magical Amalfi coast. Running along the emerald mountainside, we see glimpses of the iridescent sea below as the sun breaks through the clouds. A thin guardrail is all that separates the narrow road from the cliffs below. At particularly precarious spots, we suck in our breath, hold on to each other, and thank God that we are not the ones driving. We are free to concentrate on the amazing scenery and the expert commentary our guide provides.

"You see the yachts cruising along the coast? The Amalfi Coast is the playground for the rich and famous. Many celebrities come to these private islands to vacation."

We stop at an overlook and everyone piles out to take pictures of the once-in-a-lifetime view. A fellow passenger offers to take a photo of the four us. With the Mediterranean Sea as a backdrop, we smile as if we are having the time of our lives. We are.

As we approach our first stop, Alessandro's voice crackles through my headset.

"Now we are approaching Positano. See the cars parked along the roadside? The city is built on the cliffside and there are few places to park."

He motions to the cars lining both sides of the narrow road and when we go around the turn, the city shows itself. Positano, like the other cities along the Amalfi coast, is a vertical city. Its buildings in colors of bronze, terra-cotta, and umber hug terraced plots as the mountain plunges into the sea. It's a fairy tale landscape with the patina of centuries, a postcard photograph, a movie backdrop.

Our driver pulls into a bus parking lot at the entrance of the city. Before we unload, Alessandro explains the bus will go on ahead of us and after visiting Positano, we will take a ferry to Amalfi. This causes a moment of concern.

"No one told me we would be on a boat," Scott laments. He is prone to seasickness and avoids any type of watercraft if at all possible. Here he has no choice.

As the bus pulls away, we walk down the steep road into the city's picturesque labyrinth of stairways and narrow alleys lined with pots of bougainvillea and lemon trees. We stroll around shops and restaurants, colors bursting at each turn. Anne and I want to explore, and we lag behind until we lose sight of our guide and the voice in our earbuds fades away. Hurrying to catch up, we pass a linen shop, its walls lined with beautiful fabrics and dresses. At the entrance, an older woman is sewing on a vintage machine.

"We've got to come back here," I say to Anne.

"I know, there's so much to see!"

Alessandro gathers the group in front of the cathedral and gives us our directions, reminiscent of the countless field trips I'd organized in my career. He would have made an excellent teacher.

"You have an hour to shop or sightsee or stop at a cafe for an espresso. We will meet at the dock at 11:00. Be prompt. Our ferry leaves at 11:15. Keep your receivers turned on so we can keep in touch."

Anne and I exchange worried glances. One hour is not much time. This is exactly why we wanted to avoid a bus tour. We must move fast. Our first task is to get rid of our husbands.

"We want to do some shopping," I say. "Why don't you two walk around and find a bar or something?"

They think this is a great idea. Free at last, we prioritize.

"Let's go back to the linen shop. You still need to find a dress," Anne says.

We retrace our steps to find the woman at her vintage Nicchi sewing machine. I know she's there to lure customers in—and it worked—but it's a charming touch and another chance to practice Italian. I take my phone and translate "I like to sew."

"*Mi piace cucire*," I say. My pronunciation is way off, so I show her the words on my phone.

"*Ah, bene*! Good!" she smiles.

Through gestures I gather she does the finishing touches on the dresses on display.

"*Bellissimo!*" I say as I point to the dresses.

Anne and I glance through the display of beautiful linen dresses. I notice a dress made of the same lemon fabric that Capri Girl from our tour group is wearing, though this dress is more conservative–one piece, knee-length, buttoned up, no midriff showing. I take it and a few others to the dressing room. The lemon dress is the first thing I try on.

"What do you think?" I ask.

"Well, it's cute and it fits you well, but I can't quite see you wearing those giant lemons back home. Would you feel out of place at Target in Tucson?"

Ever practical, Anne is right. Too touristy. Besides, it makes me look like Capri Girl's mother. I slip on an apricot-hued, sleeveless A-line and I'm in love. It's the color of the sunset and the linen is light and breezy. I step out to show Anne.

"Oh, I like this one!" she says.

"Me too, but is it too light? I mean, can you see through it?" I whisper this last part.

"Step out here in front of the window... well, yes, maybe, but not *too* much if you wear neutral-colored underwear. The dress is lovely on you, and it's on sale. Get it!"

This is why women shop in packs. The saleslady wraps the apricot linen dress in tissue and puts it in the bag. With fifteen minutes to spare we dash out to find the guys. It's misting as we walk towards the designated meeting spot at the dock. My umbrella is still attached to my purse, ready to spring into action when necessary.

"Great, it's going to rain," Scott says as he eyes the ferry bobbing up and down against its moorings. "Hopefully we can find a seat in the covered area on the lower deck."

Our tour group gathers along with many others waiting for the ferry to unload. Alessandro hands out tickets and counts heads to make sure we are all here, then moves us toward the front of the crowd. It's another good teacher trick. The ferry is busier than usual this morning and he can't afford to leave anyone behind.

The last passenger disembarks and Anne and Scott head to the lower deck. Ed and I follow, but at the last minute, I change my mind.

"Let's go up. I want to see the water and the coastline," I say.

A light rain splashes against my face as we climb the stairs to the upper level. We find a covered spot with access to the open upper deck. Capri Girl and her husband sit in front of us. They are both on their phones as we pull away from the dock and move into open water. I press my nose against the foggy window, straining to see the famous Amalfi coast. Designated as a World Heritage Site, this coastline is one of the most scenic places in the world. Now we get the privilege of seeing it in panoramic splendor from the water. Wanting to see more, I move to the open deck. It's too crowded for an umbrella, but I don't want to miss this once in a lifetime opportunity.

Misty clouds have turned the typically sapphire water into shades of slate and silver. I am viewing a landscape that has been unchanged for centuries. Once only accessible by donkey paths, ancient watercolor villages cling to the mountainside, one after the other, as if displayed in an artist's studio. Cathedral domes reach to the sky. Remains of ancient defense towers dot the shore; their somber shapes testify to the struggles this coastline has seen as its inhabitants fended off pirates and other aggressors through the centuries. Now the only invaders are welcomed tourists who instead of plundering, leave money behind at restaurants and shops.

I stand at the rail snapping one breath-taking picture after another until the last possible moment when the dock at Amalfi is in sight. A light rain kisses my face and I'm drizzly wet, but somehow, I don't mind. Back at my seat, I notice Capri Girl and her husband are still on their phones. As we bump into port, she puts on her hat and scans her reflection in the window before she departs.

Our guide Alessandro grants us several hours in Amalfi and the first order of business is to find a place for lunch. Many restaurants vie for our attention. Servers stand in front of menu boards to entice tourists into their establishments. Each board advertises the same tourist fare—lasagna, pizza, carbonara, risotto, along with pictures of each dish. We choose one that has an inviting outdoor area that's covered to avoid the still drippy weather. On the table I notice a hand lettered sign propped between two wine corks:

*La vita e troppo breve*
*per manglare e bere male!*
(Life is too short to eat and drink poorly)

These few words sum up Ed's philosophy of life. Or at least his mindset when traveling. He seems to carry a food map around in his brain. If you ask him about a trip he took to Yellowstone with his family when he was ten years old, he'll say "We stopped at a place right outside of the park and they had pancakes as big as my plate!" And the trip to Florida with his family one year for Christmas? "That was the first time I ever had prime rib."

Now an adult, he loves to sample local delicacies. On our first trip to Venice, he was determined to try squid ink pasta. When the waiter brought out the black spaghetti, the rest of us starred and watched as he savored each bite. It turned his lips and teeth black for several hours.

Along the Amalfi Coast he wants to get as much fresh seafood as he can. Anne spent part of her childhood in New England so she's excited to try the seafood as well. Not me. My family's idea of seafood was fish sticks Mom purchased from the frozen food section. I especially have an aversion to eating anything that looks like it was just pulled kicking and screaming from the ocean.

We sip wine and look over the menu. Ed and Anne order seafood risotto, Scott and I choose more familiar options. When our food arrives, I watch as the server places steaming plates in front of Ed and Anne. Black-shelled clams—some open, some not—scallops, shrimp with legs still attached, and something with tentacles, top the creamy risotto.

"Want one?" Ed asks as he waves a shrimp in my face.

Its little black eyes stare at me and inches-long, wispy pink antenna droop down its sad little face. It didn't use to be bright pink, but now that it's cooked it matches the color of my Cajun Shrimp toenails.

"Ah, no."

Ed and Anne dig in, prying things out of shells and peeling the skins off the shrimp. I'm happy to see that my carbonara comes with no moving parts.

After a leisurely lunch, we stroll around the shops and take in sights and sounds of Amalfi.

"I want to buy a hat," Ed announces as we pass one shop.

So, here's another thing about my husband. He's obsessed with hats. When we were in England, he bought a flat, newsboy-style hat. He wears it everywhere; in fact, he's wearing it now. But today, it seems he wants an Italian hat. He tries on several and decides on a gray-woven fedora style with a flipped-up brim in the back. He puts his English hat in the shopping bag and wears his new hat out of the shop.

"What do you think?" he asks.

*A hat does not an Italian man make*, I think to myself, but he's happy and I'm glad to see the English hat taking a break.

"I like it!" I smile. Actually, it's kind of cute.

Anne and I stop to admire the vibrant colors and patterns of the ankle length, flowy palazzo pants blowing in the breeze in front of one shop.

"We should get these. Oh, look! They come with matching midriff tops," she giggles as she holds up the ensemble. She returns them to the rack, but as we prepare to leave Amalfi, I glance back over my shoulder. The pants wave a sad goodbye. *You missed your chance,* they seem to say.

We have one more stop on our day trip. Our bus meets us in Amalfi and we drive away from the coast and upward to the alpine village of Revello. It's cooler here, and the air is fresh with the scent of pine. Once again, parking is limited and the bus must stop outside of the city. The sky is clear now and I'm tired of dragging my umbrella around. As we get ready to deboard, I leave it on the seat.

Revello has an entirely different feel from the coastal towns of Positano and Amalfi. We hike up the road to the city and Alessandro gives us a brief history through our earphones before turning us loose to explore. It's the perfect place to end our tour. With fewer tourists, visitors can relax and take in the views of the ocean from the mountaintop. Revello is famous for its terraced gardens and summer music concerts. There is an artsy, relaxed vibe to the city; the shops and eateries we pass are not clamoring for attention.

We stop to watch a wedding party as they leave the cathedral. Young women in crimson ball-gowns hold bouquets and line both sides of the stairs. Little girls in white ruffles burst from the cool, dark cathedral to run and play among the guests. I wanted to stay long enough to see the bride, but it's time for us to get back to the bus. I linger, happy to have had this reminder that these towns are not just stops on a tourist itinerary. Real people live and work and get married here.

It's been a packed-agenda day and our tour group is more than ready to leave at the designated time. Our foursome returns to our spots in the back of the bus in time to see Capri Girl and her husband climb on. Her tote bag is overflowing with purchases and she is carrying another large to-go beverage cup with her. She removes her Capri hat and places it carefully on the luggage rack above her, then moves up and down the aisle until she has found spots for her packages in the racks above other passengers. Once settled, she and her partner continue their phone browsing. I haven't heard them talk to each other all day, but then again, I wasn't stalking them. Not really. I prefer to think of it as research for my next writing project.

On the two-hour journey back to Sorrento, the passengers are tired and conversations die down. Some nap. Our driver blares Italian pop music on the radio, perhaps to keep himself awake. Suddenly, I notice my umbrella is gone. It's not under the seat, but there's a small gap between the seat and the window, just big enough for an umbrella to slip through, and I realize it must have fallen into the luggage compartment, or worse, dropped all the way out onto the road. Now what? I didn't even use it today, but what if I need it later? When we get back,

I'll ask the driver to check the luggage compartment. And if it's not there?

*Let it go, Deb,* I tell myself. *You've sailed around the Amalfi coast with Mediterranean rain on your face. Travel lighter.*

I'm trying.

# More or Less
## *Più o Meno*

I think Ed's new Italian fedora is going to his head (pun intended). On the way back to our Sorrento hotel, he stops to look at the display of men's clothing featured in a shop window.

"I want to buy some shorts," he announces.

This is surprising coming from a man who seldom wants to shop for clothing, and only a few days ago was content with his polyester travel pants. Anne and Scott wait outside while we enter the store and find a table stacked with men's shorts. Ed picks up a pair, examines the tag in the waistband and heads to the check-out area.

"Wait, aren't you going to try them on?" I ask.

"What for?"

"They look small." I unfold the shorts and hold them up to his waist. "There's no way these will fit."

"It's my size. See?" He points to the numbers on the tag.

*Men.*

"You need to try them on."

Ed grabs the shorts and stomps off to the dressing room—a corner of the store that is closed off by a curtain. A few minutes later...

"These don't fit."

*Of course, they don't.*

I leave Ed standing behind the curtain in his underwear while I take the shorts back to the table and look for a larger size. I search through the piles, puzzled by the numbers in the waistbands. The sizing is different, possibly in centimeters? Ignoring the numbers, I go by sight, selecting several pairs for Ed to try. For the next few minutes, we play Goldilocks—too little, too big—until we find just right.

Ed is more easily adapting to the climate and carefree vibe of the Mediterranean coast than I am. Now I'm having second thoughts about my apricot-linen, light-weight dress that I bought in Positano. I love it, but I think it's too sheer. Here's the problem: I want to lighten up, be bold and wear the dress, but I hold back, afraid of revealing too much. In the end, my midwestern, conservative, kindergarten teacher orientation to clothing wins out. When we catch up with our friends, I pull Anne aside and express my concern.

"I need a slip."

"What?"

"A slip. You know, to wear under that dress. I'd be more comfortable wearing it if I had a little more... *coverage.* Let's send the guys on to pick up something for dinner. I want to check out that lingerie shop we passed."

Anne agrees, but is skeptical when we look at the shop window where sultry mannequins model sexy panties, bras, and negligees in an array of alluring colors and lacy fabrics.

"I don't think we'll find any slips in here," she whispers.

"It's worth a try."

But I think Anne is right. Entering the store, we find ourselves in a wonderland of Italian lingerie. Displays of panties, bras, and nighties, in styles ranging from suggestive to downright provocative, line the walls. We navigate through the racks, our eyes glancing over diminutive bits of fabric and lace. Nothing looks like a slip. We are about to sneak out when a beautiful, young Italian woman approaches.

"May I help you?" she asks.

I pause. My translator app would be useless, as I am quite certain there is no Italian word for what I am looking for. Gathering my courage, I try to explain.

"I bought a sheer dress and I need something to wear under it."

"Ah... *si, si,*" she smiles.

Anne and I exchange looks and follow the clerk to a cabinet in the center of the store. This might work out after all. They probably have the slips hidden away. The sales clerk opens a drawer and pulls out... a black lace thong.

"Perhaps something like this?"

My fingers fly to my lips as I stare at the tiny panties dangling from the young woman's fingers.

"Oh! No, no. I was looking for something with more coverage," I stammer, making a sweeping motion from my shoulder to my knee.

"*More* coverage?" She raises her perfect eyebrows, then folds the lacy fabric neatly and places it back in the drawer. It closes with a delicate but decisive click, placing me in the category of she-who-wears-sensible-undies.

"No, Madame, I think I cannot help you."

She's right. I'm beyond help. Who goes to Italy and spends an evening looking for a slip? I probably need a therapist, or I don't know, maybe a black lace thong. I look to Anne for moral support, but her lips are clenched, her shoulders are shaking, and she is inching out of the shop. Thanking the sales lady, I maintain my composure until I meet up with Anne on the sidewalk. We walk nonchalantly, holding ourselves together until the lingerie shop is well behind us, then...

"*Something like this?*" Anne holds up an imaginary thong. The giggles bubble up.

"*More* coverage???" I mimic, sending us into waves of hysterics. Tears run down our faces and we laugh so hard we must hang on to each other as we stumble along, drawing stares from the elegant *passeggiata* crowd stepping out for dinner.

Finally, I catch my breath. Oh, how long it has been since I've let go and laughed like this! Something inside has broken free and released this soul cleansing, knock me off my feet, out-of-control belly laughing. It's exactly what I need. No therapist required—not yet, anyway. And the black lace thong? No, of course not.

Then again...

Maybe the Mediterranean air is getting to me after all.

Back at the hotel, Ed and I rearrange the furniture on our tiny balcony to make room for Anne and Scott. They soon arrive, bringing chairs from their room. The night is warm and the iridescent pool below shimmers with underwater lighting. Across the courtyard, a man in his undershirt comes out on his balcony. He lights up a cigarette and its scent plays with the fragrance of bougainvillea on a soft breeze. City sounds pulse in the distance.

It is our last night in Sorrento and we gather around the outdoor table, a tradition we've had since our first trip to Europe with Anne and Scott several years ago. Rather than go out for a fancy diner, we meet up in one of our hotel rooms and relax over drinks and snacks. This evening, we dine on crackers and cheese, prosciutto and salami, as we reminisce about our adventures here: the lemon grove, Pompeii, the Amalfi Coast, the food we've enjoyed and people we've encountered. It's been a brilliant trip so far and we can't wait to see what Sicily brings.

"*Salute!*" we say, "clinking" our paper cups together.

"So, did you buy anything at the lingerie store?" Scott asks.

I choke on my limoncello as the hysteria begins again. The tee-shirted man glares at the four of us crammed onto a tiny balcony, drinking who knows what out of paper cups and making too much noise. He snuffs out his cigarette and returns to his room. Crazy American tourists.

If he only knew.

# Sicily
## Taormina, Mt. Etna, Palermo, Cefalu

*All of Sicily is a dimension of the imagination.*
*~ Leonardo Sciascia*

# The Train Ferry
## *Il Traghetto de Treno*

The smell of coffee and bacon entices us as we roll our luggage past the dining room, but we will have to be content with a quick breakfast at the train station. A driver will be here soon to take us to Naples where we catch a train to Sicily. I'm going to miss the breakfasts at Hotel Michelangelo. The hotel buffet, of course, is designed for tourists, many of them American, who expect substantial breakfasts, all-you-can-eat buffets, and getting one's money's worth.

I'd read that this varies from the way most Italians start their day. A typical Italian breakfast is not a meal to linger over, but more like a quick burst of energy to get your day started. Consisting of coffee, a bread roll with butter and jam or a flakey pastry, they eat it at home, or "on the go" at a local *pasticceria*. We arrive at the Naples train station in plenty of time to experience an authentic breakfast in person. At the centrally located food court, we secure a table that more-or-less accommodates the four of us, plus luggage.

"What do you want?" Ed asks.

"I'm not sure. I want to look at the pastries. Go ahead and I'll stay with the bags," I say.

While waiting, I observe the other patrons. The Naples train station is a hub serving tourists and Italian business people on their morning commutes. I can't wait to get a closer look at the pastry case, but it's the espresso bar that intrigues me. Customers stand in front of empty cups and put down coins. The barista then takes a cup to the machine, pulls a lever, and with a hiss of steam, fills the cup with a shot of thick, dark liquid. After swigging the high-octane brew in one gulp, commuters slam the cups back on the counter, then dash off while the barista replaces the used cup with a clean one. It reminds me of a western movie where a gunslinger bellies up to the bar and throws back a shot of whiskey, only in this scene, the Italian executives don't wipe their mouths on their designer sleeves or say "Thanks, Slim" as they mosey away.

I see Ed at the espresso bar, but he doesn't follow the protocol. He brings his cup and pastry back to the table.

"What kind did you get?" I point to his plate.

"I don't know, some kind of cream filling."

"Probably *crema pasticcera*," I conclude with a certain air of authority. I've been watching a popular baking show on television and besides, I like the way the words roll off my tongue.

When it's my turn at the pastry counter, I make my choice carefully. I've learned from experience at the Hotel Michelangelo, you can't always tell a cornetto by its cover. Sometimes there is a tempting dab of cream or chocolate on the top, luring you in, but when you bite into it, a hollow core disappoints you. I take my chances on one with a chocolate dab, hoping for the best. I'm feeling quite Italian now, but draw the line at the espresso bar. Though I'm fascinated by the machine, I'm not ready for the thick jolt of bitter caffeine. I order tea, momentarily disrupting the barista's efficient routine as he goes into the storage room to find a teapot.

Bringing my pot of tea and cornetto to the table, I get ready to savor my Italian breakfast, then hesitate. There is no silverware provided, and the pastry is too sticky to pick up. I glance around the room. Ahh... that's how you eat a cornetto. Wrapping the bottom of the flakey pastry in a napkin, I lift it to my lips and take a bite. Jackpot! The chocolate oozes out around my fingers. Breakfast perfection. But in true Italian style, this is no time to linger.

"Ooh, we'd better get going," Anne says as she glances at her phone.

I feel like a local, stuffing the last bite into my mouth and dashing off to catch a train. A sprinkling of flakey crumbs down the front of my shirt is all that remains.

There are several ways to get from Naples to Sicily—train, plane, bus, or car—but since there is no bridge from the mainland, you must cross over the sea at some point. This makes our train ride an interesting option.

"Let me get this straight." Scott squints at the departure board at our terminal. "We stay on the train until we run out of land then we get on a ferry?"

"The train gets on the ferry," Ed explains to our sea-wary friend.

"With us on it?" Scott raises his eyebrows.

"Yep."

"How does that work?"

"Not sure," Ed says.

"Sheesh! When did I sign up for this?"

"All part of the adventure."

As we board our train, I notice many empty seats in the first-class car. One couple is sitting behind us, and a man traveling solo is across the aisle a few seats ahead. I find it odd that four Italian police officers occupy seats at the front of the car.

"Why are they here?" I whisper.

"I saw on the morning news there was a major brawl after the soccer match in Naples last night. Maybe they thought there might be some disgruntled fans on board," Ed says.

That makes sense, but the young officers don't appear to be concerned. They barely look up from their cell phones as we stow our luggage in the overhead bins and settle into our seats. Before long, the train squeals and lurches. Wheels clack along the track slowly, then speed up to a pleasant rhythm. I'm falling in love with train travel. It's effortless—no need to worry about traffic or getting lost. Our seats are comfortable and the onboard lavatories are convenient. I expect the train steward will be along any moment to see if we want anything to eat or drink. Nothing to do but relax and enjoy our seven-hour ride to Taormina, Sicily.

Heading south from Naples, stucco-type apartment buildings and businesses give way to a more rural landscape. Small villages dot the gently rolling hills. Slender cypress trees stand guard around large villas in various degrees of disrepair, vacated, I presume, by the generations of wealthy families who once flourished here. More common are the modest homes and gardens—small, single story stucco dwellings plopped into yards cluttered with cars and clotheslines. Occasionally we see neat rows of olive groves and vineyards on the hillsides. The scenes pass by the train windows like a running loop from a movie backdrop. The show momentarily pauses when we enter one of the many tunnels, then resumes in technicolor as we burst back into the light.

"I thought the train attendant would have been around by now," I say.

"I know, they haven't even come to check our tickets," Anne remarks.

"Hmmm, maybe they're shorthanded today."

As we travel further south, we see glimpses of the Mediterranean and I am delighted that our windows are on the sea-side of the train. Anne brings out a deck of cards and the four of us play several games of gin rummy to pass the time. The solo traveler across the aisle leaves his seat and disappears through the doors heading to the next car. He returns moments later with some snacks, then turns his attention to his novel. The game wears on, but my stomach complains. It's well past lunchtime and the chocolate pastry I had for breakfast is nothing more than a delicious memory. The four police officers are eating lunches they've brought on board. Were we supposed to bring our own lunch? I thought our first-class accommodations on this all-day ride included meal service. I fidget in my seat.

"Is anyone else hungry?" I ask.

"Yeah, I'm surprised no one has come by to take our order," Ed says.

"I'm going to find out what is going on," I say.

"Who are you going to ask?" Ed grumbles.

"I'm not sure, but I'm not going to just sit here."

The police officers are the obvious choice, yet they seem aloof and intimidating. I point to the man behind his book.

"Him," I whisper.

Ed shrugs and swings his legs out into the aisle to allow me to pass. My muscles are stiff from sitting and I notice my feet are swollen making my polish-tipped toes look like the little piggies that went to market. Maybe I should have worn those compression socks on the plane after all, I think as I approach the reader.

"*Parla Inglese?*" I say one of the few phrases I know without consulting my translator ap.

"Yes, I'm Australian," the man answers.

"Oh, good," I sigh. "Is there any food service on this train? We thought there would be someone coming to take our order."

"Guess not," he smiles. "I heard there is a rail strike going on. They're pretty common in Italy. We're lucky they didn't cancel this trip altogether. That might be why we have a police escort."

Train strikes, rowdy soccer fans, and limited food service? This information slightly tarnishes my romantic image of rail travel. I glance at the officers, finishing their lunches, then notice the energy drink and bag of chips on the fold-down table in front of the Australian. He follows my gaze.

"I found a vending machine a few cars back," he explains. "The selection's not great, but..."

"Thanks. We'll see what we can scrounge up," I say.

I return from my reconnaissance mission, report back to my travel team and formulate a plan. The men seem helpless. It's up to Anne and I to forage for food and we teeter up the aisle, passing through two other cars until we reach the vending machine. Many of the selections are familiar—soft drinks, bottled water, Pringles, M&M's—but for some, we must look at the pictures and guess. The machine is the old-style type where you make your selection and push letter and number buttons to release the item you want and wait in anticipation as it (hopefully) falls into the access bin at the bottom. Once we figure that out, I try to insert a five-euro bill, but the machine doesn't accept it.

"What does that say?" Anne asks, pointing to the words over the slot.

"Introduce your money to the machine." I translate from my phone. "I guess I didn't introduce our money properly." I try again. "Hello, Machine, this is Money...Money, let us introduce you to Vending Machine."

In our food-deprived, travel-weary state of mind, this sends us into momentary fits of childish laughter, but this is serious business. After all, we are starving travelers in search of food. I attempt to reinsert the bill. The machine whirs, then spits the currency back out. We try several more bills but have no luck "introducing" them into the machine.

"Maybe the machine only accepts coins," Anne says.

We search our purses and come up with several euros worth of coins. The finicky vending machine gobbles up the change, then waits patiently for our selections. With limited funds, we make our choices based on what will give us the most for our money and return to our seats with two bottles of water, something that looks like bacon-flavored crackers, and a package of lemon cookies. With the addition of two squashed granola bars I'd had in my purse since Tucson, this will go down as one of our more memorable lunches of the trip.

With our do-it-yourself lunch finished, we try to resume our card game, but I've lost interest. The scenery has changed drastically from rural to coastal now that we are on the southern tip of Italy. I see glimpses of the sea and families playing in the waves and picnicking on blankets along sandy stretches. When we reach the station at Villa San Giovanni, the train slows, then grinds to a stop. There is no announcement, and at first, we think this is simply a long stop to allow passengers to get on and off, yet no one does. I panic slightly as the air conditioning and lights shut off and the temperature inside the car rises. Even more startling, the train clanks and lurches as if it is being pulled apart. Ed stands and presses his face to the window.

"We're backing onto the ferry."

"Really? How?" Scott asks.

"There must be tracks on the boat," Ed surmises.

When the transfer is complete, the PA system announces that we are free to leave the train to go on deck if we wish. Of course, I do! We scramble off the train to find ourselves in the belly of a large ship.

"Yep, look. The train has split into two sections, and we backed in on these tracks," Ed says.

"I didn't know we were going to do this!" The man from Australia says. "I can't wrap my brain 'round it. A train that gets onto a boat. This adds a whole new element to the trip, doesn't it?"

The guys continue to talk and point and figure out the mechanics, but I have other plans. The scent of fresh sea air lures me to the upper deck and I stand at the railing as we set sail across the Straits of Messina. Ed, Scott, and Anne soon join me. We take photos of our sun-kissed and windblown selves against the backdrop of the turquoise sky. The ferry cuts a trough through the deep sapphire sea leaving a trail of blueberry froth in its wake. I breathe it all in, sailing on timeless waters, happy to be counted among those who have taken to the sea in search of adventure. We near the port of Messina with mainland Italy to our backs and the green hills of Sicily rising to greet us.

After a twenty-minute ride the voice on the speaker announces we must return to our train. We are careful to get back into the same car we exited from. Soon, the ferry docks and the train rolls off—one section will go on to Palermo while we continue to Taormina. We have arrived on Sicilian soil.

When the train stops, we clamor off, luggage in tow, and enter a tiny depot at the base of a steep hill. Unlike the busy hubs we'd experienced at Rome and Naples, beautiful tile mosaics adorn the walls and floor of this quaint station. The building is deserted except for ticket office staff and a few taxi drivers standing by their cabs. It occurs to me we didn't make plans for getting to our hotel and I don't see any signs of a town.

"Where's Taormina?" I ask the nearest driver.

He smiles and points straight up. "There," he says.

It looks like we'll be taking a cab.

# When in Taormina
## Quando a Taormina

The driver crams our luggage into the trunk of his compact car.

"Hotel Isabella," Anne says as we squeeze in.

We travel up the side of the mountain along a serpentine road that is barely wide enough for one vehicle. I close my eyes and hold my breath as we meet a car head on. Both drivers stop and begin an intricate dance of back and forth ultimately inching around each other. When we reach the top of the hill, Sicily's legendary resort town fans out before us. The driver lets us off and points down a bustling pedestrian street lined with beautiful medieval buildings, shops, bars and restaurants.

"Hotel Isabella, 100 meters," he says.

We weave in and out through a mass of tourists until we find Hotel Isabella, a beautifully restored building with an elegantly furnished lobby. I'm admiring the red velvet drapes and gilded furniture when the well-manicured desk clerk appears. He glances at our road-weary foursome and plasters a rehearsed smile on his face.

"May I help you?"

"Yes, we have reservations for VanDeventer," Ed says.

The clerk studies his computer. "No, nothing here."

"Check for this name," Anne says flashing her passport.

"No, nothing."

Anne and I exchange glances as the same thought bolts through our minds. Could it be that we'd made an error in our perfect plans? It's our worst nightmare. We simultaneously dive into our carry-on bags and forage for folders that contain our reservations, train tickets, tour vouchers—the glue that holds this trip together. Anne is more organized than I, having filed her papers by date. While I'm still digging, she pulls out a paper, studies it, and lets out the breath she has been holding in.

"We're at the wrong hotel," she explains. "I remember now. Originally, we were supposed to be at Hotel Isabella, but changed plans at the last minute. We're booked at the Eurostars Hotel for the next three nights."

"Oh good, good," the clerk says with a sigh of relief. He pulls out a city map and circles our destination in thick black ink. "Here you go then."

Ed takes the map, and we are back on the street. He is our main navigator on our trips, Anne is the back-up and Scott and I are content to follow their lead. It's an arrangement that was established on our first trip together the year we went to England.

In London, Ed went into a market to buy "a few things for dinner" while the rest of us stayed outside. When he didn't return in a reasonable amount of time, we became worried. I entered the store and checked the wine section first, then headed to the deli counter, and ended up in the bread and cracker aisle. No Ed. To make matters worse, we had no phone coverage. I dashed out of the store and expressed my concerns to Anne and Scott. Of course, I was worried about my husband, yet my actual concern was that the rest of us did not know how to get from Piccadilly Circus to our flat in the Arsenal area. With Ed's uncanny sense of direction, even during underground transit, we never had to rely on ourselves. Just as panic set in, Ed returned with a bag of groceries, oblivious of the concern he'd caused, yet pleased to have his status as head navigator reinforced.

However, we are discovering things aren't always what they seem in Italy's ancient cities. Streets are often no more than paved footpaths that meander and change names every few meters. Maps are confusing and our phone's GPS "walking modes" are hard to follow as we travel on foot. After several false starts and stops, up and down the narrow, cobbled streets, we find what we are looking for.

The Eurostars Monte Tauro is a modern, white and glass building perched on the side of a cliff. After a long day of travel, I am relieved arrive, but dismayed to discover we have to descend an extensive set of stone steps to the main entrance. We bang our suitcases down step by step. The compact luggage I'd been so proud of in the Tucson airport now seems to be full of lead.

And my feet. I'd been careful to wear supportive athletic shoes for most of the trip, however, I'd worn sandals today thinking we wouldn't be walking that much. Big mistake. Now my feet are protesting. They grumble and puff out over my sandals. (How in the world do Italian women do this is stilettos?) I was relieved when we reached entrance where a taxi was unloading passengers. It seems we could have taxied to the front door if we'd had the right hotel in mind. Oh well. I hobble into the lobby.

The hotel was originally built in the 1970s for travelers who were seeking a more European experience. They had recently renovated the structure, yet it still maintains its signature modern style. Sleek white sofas, red accent chairs, and pop art adorn the glass and chrome lobby. The hotel is built on the side of a terraced hill, with the lobby on the ground level and each subsequent level sloping down towards the Mediterranean.

An attractive young woman checks us in.

"...and you must leave the keys with us when you go out."

This goes without saying as the massive, brass room keys are attached to ornate tassels that look like they belong on drapery tie-backs. No, I won't be carrying that around thank you, although it might come in handy if I were approached by a mugger. With the right aim, I think it could do some serious damage.

The glass-sided elevator barely holds the four of us plus our luggage. It offers a breathtaking view of the sea as we glide down the side of the hill and descend to our floor. A topless sunbather lounging on the pool deck does not go unnoticed.

We reach our rooms, and make plans to meet Anne and Scott in a few hours to go out for an early dinner. I shuffle into the room, drop my luggage and try to peel off my sandals. I think my feet have swollen to the point of absorbing the straps. Ed goes straight out to the balcony.

"You've got to see this," he says.

"I saw her," I smirk.

"What?"

"The sunbather who lost the top of her suit."

"Oh... No, she's covered up now. But come see this view."

I mope over to the sliding glass door, prepared to protest, but then—

By the sheer genius of the architects, each room has a private balcony with an unobstructed view of the Mediterranean. Lush vegetation covers the hillside and cascades gently down to the sparkling azure sea. The deck is equipped with a beautiful teak table and chairs and an awning that can be rolled out to shade the afternoon sun. Flower boxes filled with purple and blue blossoms and trailing vines line the railing. Hands down, the best view so far, and it's ours for the next few days.

Despite the gorgeous view from the balcony, my feet need attention. I briefly consider soaking them in the bidet. I'd read somewhere that you could accomplish this by filling it with water or simply holding your feet under the little faucet. There's that handy little towel hanging above it. But, no. No, I'm still wary of this bathroom fixture. We don't understand each other, yet I'm savvy enough to know it is to be used for other body parts. Both the bidet and I would be offended if I stuck my feet in there. I sit on the edge of the bathtub instead and run my feet under a stream of cold water.

After a quick nap, with my feet elevated on pillows, I shower off the day's travel and dress for dinner. I hold up the apricot linen dress I'd bought in Positano, hesitating only a moment before slipping it on. It's perfect. I'm longing to wear sandals to complete the look, but put on my walking shoes instead.

We head to dinner early by Italian standards, but this works to our advantage as we find plenty of options. The streets are lined with intimate cafes, their white tablecloths and candlelight designed to entice customers. We choose a picturesque spot and the maître d' directs us to a lovely table outdoors. Once seated, we notice the table is slanting downhill. (The entire city slants downhill.) If Ed or I spill our drinks, the liquid will run across the table and drench Anne and Scott.

Except, I will not spill a drop of the Aperol Spritz I just ordered. I fell in love with this sunset-colored drink on my first trip to Italy. Considered an apéritif, it's made from Aperol (a bittersweet Italian liqueur), prosecco, and club soda, and served with an orange-slice garnish. Sometimes, on a warm Arizona evening, Ed will make one for me while we watch the sunset over the mountains and I think of Italy. Now we're here! When the waiter brings our cocktails, we clink our glasses together.

"*Salute!*" we say. "Here's to our first night in Sicily."

"Hey," Anne says to me. "Your new dress is the same color as your drink!"

I beam. Now it will ever be known as my "Aperol Spritz Dress", or my "Italian Sunset Dress." I enjoy a most delicious dinner of pan-seared sea bass and fresh vegetables. The sun sinks below the horizon and soft candlelight illuminates our faces. Ah, Sicily.

We sleep late the next morning. It's a designated free day, meaning we have nothing scheduled. I am pleased that they equipped our room with an electric teapot, very European, and not a feature in most Italian hotels. I take advantage of our leisure time by fixing a cup and joining Ed on the terrace. The morning sun is dancing on the water while we watch the yachts and sailboats drift along.

After breakfast with Anne and Scott we walk, uphill of course, to the ruins of the Greco Roman theater, one of the major tourist attractions of Taormina. Retired English teacher Scott is in his element. We learn the Greeks built the theater in 403 BC, then renovated it a century later when the Romans conquered Taormina. The theater was constructed to be in harmony with its surroundings, which to me, is the beauty of the space. Air and light filter through what's left of the ancient columns. An archway stands alone, perfectly framing a magnificent view of the coast, and Mt. Etna reigns in the distance, its volcanic top crowned by an ominous white vapor. The arena where Greeks presented dramatic performances, and later, Romans cheered for the gladiator of their choice, is now used for outdoor plays and concerts.

Anne urges Scott to get up on the stage and pose "for the album," she says. He is reluctant at first, not wanting to attract attention, but before long the thespian in him comes out.

"Friends, Romans, and Countrymen," he flings his arms wide and shouts from center stage in mock theatrics as Anne clicks a photo or two. Scott pauses and looks out at an imaginary audience. He is in awe. "I taught Greek theater for years, but standing here, where it actually happened...what a validation."

We spend a leisurely morning strolling along, taking in the sights and sounds of the city. The piazza is beautiful; its stonework creates a surface worthy of a ballroom floor. We pass a caricature artist sketching a young woman posing in front of him. Some people sit on the low stone wall that offers a view of Mt. Etna and the bay; others are inspired to dance to the music of the accordion duo performing under the shade of parasol-shaped pines. Cafes line the piazza and we find a place for lunch.

"I would love something light," I say.

I glance through the menu, passing by the decadent pasta dishes and order a salad with grilled chicken and an iced tea. Our server brings a bowl of iceberg lettuce with processed chicken thrown on top and a can of a tea-like beverage. Lesson learned. When traveling in Italy, don't eat like a woman who has used up all of her Weight Watchers points for the next year and is trying to redeem herself. Remember, you're in Italy where the motto is *Life is too short to eat and drink badly.*

By afternoon, the late September sun is in full force and the Mediterranean climate is getting to me. My black slacks, "perfect for packing and they wash and dry quickly", are not so perfect now. They feel sad and they stick to my legs. And—more importantly—they are at odds with the carefree style and vibe of this city. Anne feels the same way.

"We need more dresses," I say and she agrees.

"You guys find a bar. Anne and I want to shop around."

This tried-and-true travel technique is beneficial to all parties. Like adult day care, the guys are taken care of and Anne and I get some time to ourselves. We soon find a shop that features linen attire at reasonable (i.e., tourist approved) prices. I pull a bright turquoise sun dress off the rack.

"Oh, that's cute," Anne says

"But look. The back has a cut-out lace panel and maybe you might be able to see…"

"Go for it!"

This time, I don't hesitate. I buy the turquoise dress and a cute print one as well. Anne buys one too.

"Three to three, we're even. You know, the dress wars," she says.

Later that day, we split up. Anne and Scott head out to tour the city gardens and Ed and I spend the afternoon window shopping. One store in particular catches my eye. Dare I?

"Let's go in here," I say.

"Seriously?" Ed raises his eyebrows, then smiles.

"Now. Before I change my mind." I grab his hand and lead him through the doors and up to the counter.

"May I help you?" the saleslady asks.

This time I know exactly what's in the drawers.

*You should have bought a slip...* Worry-warrior me says as we leave the shop.

*Oh, shut up,* I tell her. Besides what's in this tiny bag will take up way less space in my suitcase.

# The Wine Tour
## Il Tour del Vino

*Anni e bicchieri di vino no si contano mai.*
*Age and glasses of wine should never be counted.*
*~Italian Proverb*

A new day, a new adventure, a new driver. We have booked a small-group tour to the Mt. Etna Wine country. To avoid driving down the steep slope to the hotel, Juan picks us up at the top of the hill.

"*Buongiorno!*" he says. We make introductions and settle into the nine-passenger vehicle. "We will make one more stop to pick up our other guests, then we go."

We twist and turn down some of the same paths we had been walking along for the past few days. I had assumed they were pedestrian paths, but no. Now we are in the morning rush hour. Vespas, taxis, vans, busses, delivery trucks, and bicycles all move like a school of minnows through narrow channels. We swim along with the pack for a while, then, when Juan sees an opening, he honks and darts. There are no stop signs, no traffic lights, no markings on the ancient cobblestone roadways. I am once again relieved that we had opted not to rent a car for this vacation. To put this into terms my biology teacher husband would understand, driving in Italy is survival of the fittest and American tourists are not genetically wired for this.

Finally, we pull into a courtyard surrounded by stately trees and lavish bougainvillea bursting with pink and red blooms. It appears to have been an estate at one time, now converted into tourist housing. Four women are waiting for us. Juan checks off their names and they pile into the van. It's an interesting mix of ages traveling together in a women's tour group.

"So, we are all ready to drink some vino?" Juan asks as he merges into the stream of traffic.

"Of course!" exclaims one of our new friends.

We start to introduce ourselves when a classic Italian traffic stand-off interrupts us. Our van is descending the mountain and rounding a blind curve when an enormous tour bus meets us head-on. The bus driver honks, brakes screech, and we lurch forward slamming against our seatbelts. Then a game of chicken begins. The drivers glare at each other until Juan reluctantly concedes to the larger competitor. He backs the van just enough to allow the ridiculously large bus to inch forward around the curve. The two vehicles are so close, that, from our lower vantage point we can look up the noses of the bus tourists as they scroll through their phones in air-conditioned comfort, unaware of the drama unfolding below. Except now, Juan elicits startled views as he rolls down his window and pounds his fist on the side of the bus. He shouts a stream of Italian.

"Sorry," he smiles, turning towards us. "I may have said four... um, maybe five bad words."

Satisfied that he has made his feelings known, he rolls the window up and morphs back into our friendly neighborhood tour guide, the bus incident all in a day's work.

"Taormina means 'the mountain of the bulls'. Ancient civilizations sacrificed calves on the top of the mountain because it was closer to the gods," he says.

This bit of bloody information only slightly diminishes my love for this beautiful city.

"Do you live in Taormina?" I ask.

Juan shakes his head. "Taormina is a luxury city for tourists. It's too expensive. I live in a small town not far from here."

"How long have you been a tour guide?"

"Here, for ten years, but soon I want to return to Spain. That's where my family is."

Traffic is sparse now that we are out of the city. Stone fences outline small family homes, vineyards, and gardens. Juan leans back in his seat, one hand on the steering wheel, the other gesturing freely as he speaks.

"So, did you come across on the ferry? Every year Sicily has an election and the politicians all promise to build a bridge from Italy to Sicily, but it never happens. Why? Two things. First, the people here, they are Sicilians first, Italians second, you know? Maybe they like the separation. But I think the real reason there is no bridge is because the Mafia owns the ferry boat operations."

Juan lowers his voice and his dark eyes glance at us in the rearview mirror.

"I will tell you something. Maybe I shouldn't say this, but it is bothering me. This morning two men were in the hallway by my apartment. They guard the judge who lives next to me. They know my name and where I go each day."

I shift in my seat, unnerved by this revelation. There was a display in the gift shop at the Roman theater we toured yesterday. Small, brightly colored books titled, "Understanding the Mafia" were featured in English and several other languages. I thought the Mafia was something from another era, portrayed in movies. Apparently in Sicily, it exists.

The further we travel from Taormina, the more we see "the real Sicily" as Juan says. We wind through a town that looks deserted, yet signs of life are scattered about—children play in dirt lots, laundry flaps on rusty clotheslines, a few men sit on make-shift benches outside of a run-down market.

"Away from the tourists, the cities have no hospitals, no schools, no shopping," Juan reports. "The young people, they leave. You want a house? Here, you can buy for one euro. You don't believe me? Yes, it's true. But you must renovate the home within three years, and in the end, you live here." He gestures at the bleak town. "Think about it."

We drive around a corner and see a brilliant view of Mt. Etna, considered one of the world's most active volcanoes.

"See the cloud at the top? That is vapor, the volcano is letting off steam. This is a good thing. It means there is no big activity. The volcano is like a bottle of Champagne, you know? If you let the pressure out slowly, it's ok. If it stays bottled up...kaboom." Juan explodes his hands off of the steering wheel.

"So, what is the evacuation plan?" Scott asks.

"Ha! This is Sicily...nothing works here. There are no plans. They would try to get boats to the people I suppose but..." his voice trails off. I think back to plaster casts of the people of Pompeii trying to escape Mt. Vesuvius.

"Mt. Etna erupts once every 400 years," he continues.

"When was the last eruption?" one of our traveling companions asks.

"409 years. So, when we get to the winery, drink fast, my friends," he jokes.

"So why do the people stay here?"

"This is their home; generations of families have made their lives here. And the volcano that destroys, later gives back. See the stone fences? They are built of lava stone. And the soil from the volcanic ash produces the best fruits and vegetables. The wine made from the grapes grown on this hillside...mwahh." He kisses his fingertips. "You will see."

As if on cue, we are in the gently rolling foothills of Mt. Etna wine country. We stop at a small, family-owned winery. It is a pleasant, sunny day. The air temperature is refreshing, a few degrees cooler than the hot humid air in Taormina that has prompted me to buy three sundresses, one of which I'm wearing today. The son of the vineyard owner greets us with glasses of wine and we gather with several other guests on the terrace overlooking the vineyard. A perfect warm breeze blows across the vineyard, vines bend with amethyst-hued fruit, glasses of wine clink, and friends are made. This is why people fall in love with Italy.

The young man stands at the edge of the gathering and tells the story. We learn his father started the vineyard in the 1980s. Prior to that time,

Sicilians were making wine to export. The aim was quantity over quality. Workers labored in the vineyards for meager pay and a daily liter of wine. Many of the vineyards died out as young people moved away to find better opportunities. But thirty or forty years ago, spurred on by the booming tourist industry, an interest in reviving the wineries emerged. The focus turned to cultivating the best wines and employing the latest knowledge about winemaking to produce a quality product. Many of the wineries now sell wines under their own labels to elite markets worldwide.

"How is the wine?" our guide asks. "I should warn you; Sicilian wine is stronger, higher in alcohol content than Italian wine, which is table wine to drink throughout the day without getting drunk. But no worries. Sicilian grapes are full-bodied, enriched with the soil of the volcano and we add no extra sulfates. So, drink up. No headaches tomorrow!"

We move in small groups through the guts of the winery. No Lucille Ball grape-stomping here. Instead, we are in the center of a state-of-the-art, stainless-steel refinery. Our guide takes us step by step through the process, but I am more interested in getting back to the dining room for the promised light lunch and wine tasting.

Our driver Juan motions for us to join him at a table and seats us with the four women from our group. Soon the server brings plates of cheese, olives, roasted red pepper, baked eggplant, and a rustic loaf of bread served with olive oil. He holds up a white wine, describes it, and pours a generous splash into the wine glasses in front of each of us. A Sicilian table loaded with food and wine is the perfect setting for getting to know our new travel companions.

Heather is dressed in shorts, sandals and a casual, embroidered top. With her honey-colored hair worn loose around her shoulders she has a bohemian look about her. We learn she is from Liverpool, a single mother of three children.

"I divorced my husband when the kids were grown. Yes, all three have the same dad," she is quick to point out. "He's a jerk, but I'm not a floozie."

We all laugh and sip our wine. The eggplant is delicious, but I slide my olives onto Ed's plate.

"Are you traveling by yourself then?" Anne asks.

"Yeah, I quit my job three months ago. I'm traveling for a year, then I start my new job working for an oil company in Dubai."

Traveling solo for a year? Working in Dubai? I find this to be utterly brave and fascinating. Just then our wine steward pleasantly interrupts with another variety of white wine to describe. He adds a second glass to each place setting, and the conversation continues. I drizzle some olive oil onto a slice of bread.

"So, are you traveling alone?" I ask Tammy, the physical therapist from California sitting across from me.

"I was going to come with my son, but at the last moment, he canceled. I came anyway." Tammy readjusts the backpack she wears like armor across her chest. "I'm off to a rough start, though."

Tammy was on the train ferry from Italy to Sicily only a few days after we were. Like everyone else, she had gone up to the deck of the ferry to enjoy the ride, but when it was time to get back on the train, she got on the wrong section and ended up in Palermo. Finally, she was able to get to Taormina to join up with her tour group, although getting her luggage back was a nightmare.

"That's why I'm carrying my essentials with me wherever I go," she says patting her pack. I couldn't help noticing the tiny locks on each zippered compartment. Tammy is a nervous sort of traveler, yet, I admired her courage to continue on this trip on her own. Hopefully, the rest of her travels would go smoothly. Maybe another glass of wine would put her in better spirits. The sommelier describes our next selection and pours samples of the ruby-red wine into our glasses.

While we enjoy the antipasto selections, Ed, Anne, Scott, and I answer questions about our backgrounds, mentioning this is the third European trip we had done together.

"You four remind me of my parents. In fact, my mother's name is Debbie." the young woman sitting next to Scott says.

This puts me in a different generation than Andrea, but she adores her parents so I take this comparison as a compliment. I noticed Andrea when we pulled up to the villa to gather this group of women into our tour. Tall, dark-complected, and striking with her close-cropped ebony hair, she wears a stylish turquoise tank top, cream-colored palazzo pants, and bold earrings. Andrea just turned thirty-six and is celebrating her birthday by traveling for a month until she begins her new position as an attorney in New York.

One of our new companions remains a mystery. She smiles and nods as she follows the conversation, yet offers few comments. She is a petite, young woman and we know only that her name is Sophia, she is from Singapore, and she prefers to travel alone.

Our fourth and final wine sample has arrived. Another bold red. By now, our group members seem like old friends. We laugh and enjoy each other's company over good food and glasses of wine.

I look around the table at the plethora of empty wine goblets—eight guests with four glasses each. It was only a tasting, a sampling, right? Besides, what did our guide say about Sicilian wine? Something about the alcohol content...enjoy the wine...no headaches...volcanoes erupting...drink fast? It all seems a bit foggy to me now, like the vapor that has been swirling around the top of Mt. Etna for 409 years. But who's counting?

# Hello Palermo
*Ciao Palermo*

It's a travel day. With my bags packed, I fix a cup of tea and step onto the balcony. It's going to be hard to say goodbye to Taormina, Sicily's jewel-box city. Ed joins me and we sit side by side watching a sailboat glide across the bay past private yachts, anchored overnight. Wisps of cotton clouds streak the blue sky. I close my eyes and inhale the warm, salt-tinged air.

"I wish we could stay longer." I reach over and take Ed's hand.

"Me too," he squeezes back.

Nevertheless, we want to see more. *The resort towns are for tourists. They are not the real Sicily;* Juan had said yesterday. Today we are off to Sicily's capital city hoping to broaden our view.

There is no direct way to Palermo. We have a first-class reservation on the train to Messina, then we will take a commuter train for the rest of the journey. We arrive early at the Taormina station only to discover our train is running late. Ed and Scott find a bench and corral the luggage while Anne and I pace the platform checking the arrival board for updates. Police officers, a man and a woman, approach.

"Passports?" the woman asks. After a quick flip through each of our documents, she hands them over to her partner to be scanned.

The officers ask a few questions about where we are going and where we've been (I leave out the part about the trip to the lingerie shop), then check our tickets and move on to repeat the procedure with the few others waiting on the platform. This is the second time we've seen police officers in and around trains in Sicily.

Finally, ours arrives. We board, find seats and settle back to enjoy a brief, pleasant ride along the coast. The two Italian women sitting across the aisle give the first sign we are leaving the resort areas. Unlike the young, show-case women we saw parading around Sorrento and Taormina, these women wear casual clothing and appear to be about our age. Anne nudges me and smiles. It's refreshing to see Italian women who look kind of like us. The women speak in quick bursts of Italian and I strain to catch a word or two. One laughs and tucks a strand of her gray/black hair behind her ear. She glances over and I realize I must have been staring.

"*Ciao*, hello," I say.

"*Buongiorno. Parla Inglese?*" she asks.

"*Si. Americano.*"

"*Ah, bene.* Silvia and Mona," she smiles and points herself and her friend.

Anne and I introduce ourselves and we strike up an Italian/English conversation. Though sketchy—I still rely on my translator app—we discover Silvia and Mona are educators, dedicated to learning English so they can teach others. Silvia, the more fluent of the two asks where we are going.

"Palermo for three days," I say.

The women exchange looks, then converse in a short flurry of Italian. Mona holds up her bag and they laugh.

"What did she say?" I ask.

"She said to be careful in Palermo."

Mona nods, pantomimes a purse-snatching, and they laugh again.

So, this is our introduction to Palermo. Not 'be sure to see this' or 'you will love it there' or 'it's a beautiful city.' Our only words of advice from the Italian women are to hold on to your purses.

Purses. The Achilles heel of all women travelers. If you get this piece wrong, you will regret it for your entire vacation. Anne and I worry over this before every trip. On our previous journey to Italy, we talked ourselves into purchasing specialized travel handbags. After extensive research we bought ones with slash-proof straps, scan-proof compartments and locking zippers. Prepared for any type of weather, we opted for the larger size to stow a travel umbrella or light jacket. Intent on color-coordinating with our travel wardrobe, Anne's was teal, and I bought the same bag in coral.

After the first day in Milan, we knew we'd made a mistake. The same zippers that clicked onto hidden brackets to keep pickpockets at bay, also made it impossible to retrieve passports or sunglasses without going through complicated finger calisthenics. To make matters worse, the enormous bags hung like teal and coral albatrosses around our necks and bounced on our tummies and hips as we carried them cross-body style.

"Never again," Anne had said.

So, this time, I'm carrying the small shoulder bag I had used in England, the one that is not large enough for an umbrella (explaining why I had to hook it onto the bag's strap the day we went to Amalfi), and Anne brought a petite one her travel-savvy sister-in-law had given her.

"But the straps aren't slash-proof. Do you think I'll be OK?" Anne asked on one of our pre-trip phone calls.

I told her I thought it would be fine. We'd been on two European trips and had yet to encounter slashers.

Our train stops in Messina and we say goodbye to the Italian women. Though we are not in Palermo, we clutch our valuables close as we disembark. We have about forty-five minutes before we board our next train, and not wanting a repeat of the ride from Naples where we traveled all day without food or water, I dash to the station's cafe/convenience store. Here I find the obligatory countertop espresso bar where travelers stand, throw back shots, and dash off. This slurp-and-go coffee drinking experience still fascinates me, yet I think Americans who are used to their Grande-skinny-vanilla-latte-with soy milk-no whip, would not go for this. I pass up the espresso bar and buy a bottle of water and two (of what looks like) power bars and join Ed, Scott, and Anne on the platform.

"It's only two and a half hours, I doubt we'll starve," Ed says, eyeing the snacks.

We board our train and plop down on plastic seats that are molded to conform to most (not all) backsides. We are fortunate to find a place to sit and overhead space for our luggage. Travelers who board later need to stand, holding on to the overhead bars for support. I pass the time observing our fellow passengers. Two teenaged girls have taken the seats in front of us, and a young man in black jeans and a dark hoodie slouches in his seat across the aisle. As the porter comes to check tickets, he tells the young man he must wear a face mask. The young man pulls the neck of his sweatshirt over his mouth and nose, but no. The officer informs him that if he doesn't have a mask, he will need to get off at the next stop. In the post-COVID world masking is required on trains, yet the porter's reaction seems harsh. I search my purse for an extra mask, but one of the teenaged girls finds one first and hands it to the dark-clad man, saving him from deportation.

"*Grazie*," he mutters, then returns his attention to his phone.

The train stops at many small towns along the way, waiting a few minutes at each as travelers get on or off. We know we are getting closer to Palermo when rural landscapes give way to urban scenes. Soon, we arrive at the terminal. Unlike the quaint station at Taormina, the Palermo Centrale station is a major transportation hub for Sicily. We exit the train into a crowd of travelers and business people stepping out into the center of Julius Caesar Square, aptly named for the grandeur of the city center. Looking back at the station, I take in the magnificence of this multi-level structure, with its arched windows and doorways and classic columns, a masterpiece of eighteenth-century architecture setting high expectations for adventures to come.

It's a quick cab ride to the hotel. Along the way I gather first impressions of this major city, a far cry from the resort towns of Sorrento and Taormina.

Sicily's capital city is a melting pot of cultures with a diverse and turbulent history. Because of its position on the Mediterranean Sea, Palermo has the reputation of being one of the most conquered cities in the world, each passing culture having left its mark.

Our hotel is a large, modern structure overlooking the Gulf of Palermo on the Northern coast of Sicily. We enter its grandiose lobby and weave our way through a convention of Italian businessmen and women wearing nametags. We wait in a long line to check in, then the elevator takes us to the fourth floor. Our room is small, but well-appointed for international tourists. The bathroom features a sleek glass-and-tile shower with a waterfall showerhead. Accustomed to seeing a bidet in the bathroom, I notice where it is to avoid any further late-night mix-ups.

I walk across the room and pull back the drapes, but instead of a deck with a glorious view of the Mediterranean, we have a small window that overlooks the backsides of dozens of apartment buildings. I notice a man in a sleeveless, white tee shirt draping clothes on a rack that extends out from his tiny balcony. In fact, it must be laundry day because I see an assortment of shirts, dresses, bras, and undies flying like flags from other apartments. If

I stand here long enough, I will know intimate details about our neighbors based on their laundry.

But for now, it's time to join Anne and Scott for a late lunch. Our hotel has only two small elevators, not nearly enough to accommodate the number of guests they serve, and we wait several minutes for one to stop at our floor. When the door opens, a woman dressed in taupe slacks and a white silk blouse looks up from her phone and moves over to make room for our foursome. A hint of her perfume lingers behind. On the next floor down, the door opens to reveal a large man waiting to get on. He takes a tentative step in and I move over.

"We'll make room," I say.

The fragrant woman in taupe springs into action. She holds up a manicured hand, plants her Gucci-clad heels, and assumes the stance of a traffic cop.

"NO!" she blurts.

The man backs out sheepishly, and the door closes in his startled face.

"Too many people?" I say pointing to the elevator capacity sign.

"No," she says. Then she motions to show the man's large stomach and laughs. Somewhat shocked at her insensitive, but accurate appraisal of the situation, I watch as she repeats her imitation. It seems we have learned a valuable lesson in Italian elevator etiquette. Regardless of the posted capacity limit, if your stomach is large, be prepared to travel alone.

Because they reserve the dining room for convention attendees, our only option for lunch is the poolside cafe. We find an umbrella table and enjoy the pleasantly warm afternoon. Couples and families relax in the pool while cabana boys bring drinks to sunbathers. The limited menu caters to American tastes—pizza, burgers, salads. The gin and tonics and Aperol Spritzes put us all in a pleasant mood.

"Our Hop-On-Hop-Off bus tour is tomorrow," Anne reminds us.

"Where do we catch it?" Scott asks.

"I don't know but think it would be a good idea to take a walk after lunch and find out," Anne says.

Our travel agent had suggested this tour to get an overview of the city. With our tickets, we could join the tour at any stop and exit the bus at points of interest throughout the day. However, we have very little information about how this works. After lunch, three of us pull out our phones (Scott prefers a simple, phone-free travel existence) and google "Where to catch the Hop-on-Hop-Off bus in Palermo." This results in different opinions about where to go, so we spend a great deal of time wandering around.

"This way," Anne takes the lead pointing to a paved walkway between tall brick buildings. Leafy green foliage and flowers fill pots along the path and spill from window planter boxes. A pair of murals catches our attention. The artist has painted two faux window scenes on a brick wall complete with real, green weathered shutters attached to the sides of each. If it wasn't for the caricature Italian women gazing out, you would think they were actual windows. The painter has portrayed neighbors who have flung open their windows to have a visit. One woman is in her kitchen holding a blue china coffee cup, an orange tabby cat at her side. She has bold red hair and exaggerated red lips. Pink painted panties and lace stockings hang from an authentic clothesline strung under her window ledge. Her neighbor, a raven-haired woman with scarlet heart-shaped lips is leaning on a pillow, arms crossed in front of her revealing an ample bosom spilling from her camisole. Her head turns towards her neighbor as if to catch the latest gossip. The women come to life in this masterpiece of Palermo street art.

The path empties into a lush park, once the courtyard of a fine home now converted into luxury apartments. Here we find what we are looking for—a bus stop sign with the "Hop on Hop Off" logo—and hope we can find it again in the morning. We retrace our steps back to the hotel to rest and freshen up, agreeing to meet for an evening stroll and a light dinner.

At dusk we head out on foot from our hotel in the direction the taxi had taken us earlier in the day. We were sure we'd passed some places that might have what we were looking for. However, what we thought was a cafe turns out to be nothing more than a convenience store. The parking lot is full of young people on scooters and we decide to keep searching.

"This looks interesting," Ed says.

I turn to see an elaborate archway constructed of posts and wire, lit with what looks like Christmas lights. Since it is September, I'm guessing they're not. I hang back.

"Is this even a street? It looks more like an alley. Is it safe?" I ask.

"We wanted to experience Palermo," he answers.

"I know, but..."

"Come on."

With some hesitation, we follow. This is not a tourist destination. There are no planters of flowers here and the pavement is littered with cigarette butts, beer bottles, and overflowing trash cans. In place of street art caricatures, real life neighbors sit in front of their apartments to take advantage of the cooler evening temperatures, their shapes silhouetted as amber light sneaks through open windows and doorways. A group of young girls on bicycles catches Anne's attention. They ride down the street, laughing and shouting to a group of boys running behind them.

"I love it. Those girls have the bikes and the power. Someday they'll trade bicycles for scooters and boys will still try to catch up," Anne laughs and I smile thinking about the stiletto-mini-skirt-scooter-riding woman that turned heads in Sorrento.

The air is humid and warm, trapping in rich, earthy smells of recently cooked dinners. Several young men loiter on the corner; cigarette smoke swirls around them, then disappears into the dim light of a streetlamp. Curious eyes follow as we pass. Snippets of recent conversations haunt me. *The mafia runs all the ferries... nothing works in Sicily... hold on to your purse.* I feel uneasy and move closer to Ed.

"I don't like this. I want to go back to the hotel," I whisper.

"Deb..."

"No, I want to go back."

Ed shrugs and takes the next street to the hotel.

We end up at the poolside cafe where the evening crowd—tourists and business people — gather around festive tables. Underwater lights create an azure glow on the bodies of late-night swimmers. The server brings us drinks and an assortment of olives, nuts, and potato chips. We sip our cocktails and discuss our adventures and misadventures, a pleasant way to end a long day of travel. And yet, something is bothering me.

"That walk scared me," I say.

"I wasn't really afraid, but it's not the kind of scene they put on the travel brochures," Anne says.

"Well, it made me nervous. I didn't like it."

"Why not? It's part of Sicily," Ed says.

I glance at a high wall, landscaped and lush, that surrounds the hotel's glamorous pool and separates us from the neighborhood we had just walked through. A neighborhood where Real people relax after work and fix dinner and visit with neighbors. Where children play in the street and laundry hangs from window ledges. Where Real Palermo lives. Why was I so uncomfortable there?

Ah, yes. I recognize it now. The Bubble— disguised as a wall and a fancy hotel—has followed me to Palermo. The minute I was faced with an unfamiliar situation, I retreated back to my comfort zone. Exactly what I hoped I wouldn't do on this trip.

But watch out Bubble. I'm on to you.

# On and Off
*Acceso e Spento*

At breakfast, I notice Anne is wearing one of her new dresses.

"Oh, that looks nice on you, and it's going to be a good day for a light, breezy dress. My phone says 90s and humid," I say.

"I can't do it," Anne whispers.

"What?"

"I can't wear this dress in public."

"Anne..."

"No, I'm serious. When I stand in the sun, you can see through it."

"It's the same style as the one I'm wearing, just a different color."

"Well, you're braver than me. I'm not wearing this."

Anne's mistaken, I'm not brave. My reaction to yesterday's stroll through the dark alley is proof. So today, I'm determined to step out of my comfort zone and battle The Bubble. The gauzy, floral blue dress that I purchased in Taormina (a dress that may or may not be slightly see through) is my weapon of choice. I do a test, walking past the large, sunny windows on the way to the buffet. No alarms go off and I'm pretty sure no one in the dining room cares what I'm wearing; it's the pastries that are on full display. I select a couple, adding some fruit and a few slices of prosciutto to the plate to balance out my breakfast. When I return to the table, I raise my eyebrows at Ed's piled-high plate and large cup of espresso.

"You're supposed to use a demitasse cup for that," I say.

"Yeah, but this way I don't have go back for refills. Besides, I'm not a *demitasse* kind of guy." Ed picks up his mug and sticks out his pinkie finger. "How's this?"

Anne and Scott snicker.

"Don't encourage him," I say. "If he drinks that entire cup, he'll *literally* hop on and off the bus."

"Maybe we should all caffeine up. I don't understand this Hop-On-Hop-Off tour anyway," Scott says.

"Me neither, but we'll figure it out, assuming we find the bus stop again," Anne says.

After breakfast, we go back to our rooms to gather what we need for the day. When we meet in the lobby, I notice Anne has changed into capris and a top, but say nothing. We find the bus stop and are trying to decipher the schedule when we hear a loud rumble followed by a whiff of diesel fumes.

"How will we know this is the sightseeing bus?" Scott asks.

"Oh, I think we'll know," Anne laughs.

A large double-decker vehicle careens around the corner. It's Elmo-red with a canary-yellow railing around the open-air top level, looking as if it came from Sesame Street. The words *'Sightseeing Palermo'* scream in yellow and pink puffy letters, and abstract scenes of the city swirl in shades of purple, orange, green and blue around the sides. When the bus clatters to a stop, I half expect to see Big Bird driving and one of the Muppets taking our tickets, but a human in black slacks and a white shirt scans our passes.

"These are good for all day for both the Red and the Blue Line." She smiles and hands us maps and little packets of earbuds for the audio tour. I've wanted to ride on the top of a double-decker bus ever since our trip to England. Here's my chance.

My travel companions are not as enthusiastic, but follow me up the stairs. A few single seats remain, scattered among the crowd of early morning tourists. Before we split up, we agree to stay on the tour for one complete loop around the city before deciding where we might like to hop off for exploring. With the help of the man sitting next to me, I plug in my headset and adjust the settings to

English. Soft, classical music plays through the earbuds and a cheery voice welcomes me to Palermo:

*Along the avenue are beautiful Jacaranda trees forming a canopy. Originally from South Africa, these trees do very well in the climate here. They begin their blooming season in early summer and continue their show of lavender flowers for several months. The Jacaranda tree symbolizes wisdom, rebirth, wealth and good luck.*

Sitting at tree-top level, I'm delighted by the petals that float onto my hair and land in my lap like purple confetti. We're off to a grand start. I look back at Ed, and wave like a debutante in a homecoming parade.

*...and on our right, we have La Vucciria, an ancient bazaar area and neighborhood in the Castellammare quarter here in central Palermo. The word vucciria is the Sicilian word for confusion, an apt name for the sound of the hawkers proffering their wares in the market. Here you can find produce, cafes, and perhaps a souvenir or two to take home.*

This entices several people to hop off the bus and Anne and Scott find seats across the aisle from me.

"Looks interesting. We might want to come back here for lunch." I say over the narrator's voice. Anne nods.

"Too touristy," the man beside me blurts. I want to remind him that we are in fact on a tour bus—being touristy is the whole point.

*Up ahead, is the Teatro Massimo Opera House. Designed by the celebrated Italian architect Giovan Battista Filippo Basile, it was completed in 1897, The Teatro is the largest opera house in Italy and is world renowned for its breathtaking architecture and perfect acoustics. You will want to book a tour or purchase tickets for one of the seasonal performances.*

By now the sun is in full force and I'm thinking I should have worn a hat. Even so, I'm enjoying my bird's-eye view. The narrator talks about the next attraction, the Palermo Cathedral, *a must-see for anyone visiting Palermo,* but I'm distracted by a conversation Scott is having with some people who just hopped on. As they walk past, one man notices Scott's cap.

"Empire Ranch! In Arizona? I've been there. Are you a rancher?" the man asks, pointing at Scott's boots.

"No, I toured it when visiting my friends in Arizona." Scott nods towards us. "My wife and I have a farm in Indiana."

The two men continue their conversation and I turn my attention back to the tour...

*Many architectural styles characterize the Palermo Cathedral because of its long history of additions and alterations....*

I don't see a cathedral. Did I miss it? I lean forward and my dress sticks to my back while I fan my face with the map. The bus maneuvers through multiple lanes of baffling traffic and turns onto a magnificent avenue lined with tall, historic buildings. Cascades of bougainvillea and lush, lacy vines flow from elaborate ironwork balconies.

*You might wonder about the Moorish-head flower pots on these balconies and throughout Sicily. This tradition is based on a local legend.*

Anne looks up and points. We saw these types of pots in shops in Taormina—pairs of royal heads, a man and a woman, lavishly decorated, sometimes light skinned, sometimes dark. One store dedicated an entire wall to a display of refrigerator magnets featuring the heads. Anne, an avid souvenir-magnet collector was curious about them.

*There are many versions of the story, but one legend says that in the city of Palermo lived a beautiful girl who loved to tend the garden on her balcony. One day a handsome Moor passed by and the two fell in love and began a romance. However, the young woman found out that the man had a wife and children waiting for him in the Far East. In a fit of jealousy, she cut off the man's head while he was sleeping. In one account, the woman was so distraught at what she'd done; she killed herself.*

*In another rendition, she used the head of the Moor as a pot where she planted herbs, and so it was that on her balcony grew a lush plant of basil. Inspired by the legend, other women fashioned Moorish-head planters out of pottery perhaps, to remember a love lost, or more likely to warn wayward husbands.*

*And on the right...*

The voice goes on, yet I am trying to process the severed head story. This legend would *not* make a good Disney movie. Well, it would be OK right until the adultery part—then there's the decapitation scene to deal with. I suppose the right theme song could make it work. I had considered buying a small pair of pots to take home, or perhaps magnets, but after hearing the gruesome backstory, I decided no.

On the other hand, I've had trouble coaxing the basil in my Tucson garden to thrive...

At the next stop, our foursome huddles. We have completed the loop and decide to ride a little more and exit at the cathedral that was mentioned. The narrated script replays. We pass the purple trees and the market again, hopping off at the stop just before the balconies of severed-head flowerpots.

"So where do we go from here? Where's the cathedral?" Ed looks at a city map posted on a busy corner.

"Is this it?" Scott points to a church across the street, and we head in that direction.

The doors are wide open and we go inside, but it is obviously not what we are looking for. The building is small and unadorned. There are no throngs of tourists, only a few locals sitting in pews. A woman walks to the altar and lights a small candle, then bows her head and makes the sign of the cross. We sneak out and study the brochure again. The maps are confusing; we had not done our homework, and we didn't expect to navigate the city on our own.

"I think we need to catch the Blue Line to take us to the cathedral," Anne says. "Why don't we stop for lunch while we figure this out."

We've missed the stop for the Vucciria Market, so we search for something that is open in this part of town. This proves to be challenging as it is a few minutes before noon and many places are closed.

Sicilians prefer a late lunch. We notice a young woman setting up chairs and umbrellas and ask if we can sit and wait until the café opens. She shrugs and nods.

While we wait, Anne and Ed spread out the map and dig in.

"Yeah, we need to ride back to the central station and catch the Blue Line," she says.

"Then we walk up here?" Ed traces a line with his finger.

"Looks like it."

"Is this the cathedral we heard about on the tour?"

"I think so...hopefully..."

The waitress returns with menus and even though the kitchen is not quite open and her English is limited, she takes our order and does her best to make sure we have lunch. We decide to hop back on the bus so we can return to the starting point and catch the other line. The late afternoon sun is scorching now and we take seats on the lower level which, we discover, is not air-conditioned. As we approach the avenue of balconies (for the second, or is it third time?), I yank out my earbuds and toss them onto the seat. Despite my gauzy dress, sweat is running down my back, I can barely breathe, and I think if I hear that head story again, I'm likely to throw up. Now I know why they call it a Hop-off bus.

That's exactly what I do when the bus returns to the station. I can't bear the thought of getting on another bus to find a cathedral or anything else for that matter. Judging by the expressions on my travel companions, they feel the same way.

"Let's walk back," Ed suggests.

We all agree and trudge along the sidewalk in silence. The day was a disappointment. We hopped on the bus; we hopped off, on and off, but we experienced the treasured sights of Palermo only from a distance. Now that we are off the infernal bus, there is a refreshing breeze and we walk in the shade of tall buildings in the heart of the city. Anne and I drop a few steps behind the guys.

"What did you think?" I say.

"Well, it wasn't what I was expecting. It was too hot and we couldn't figure things out. Maybe we should have done some research on Palermo. We weren't ready for it."

"The next time we're in Palermo…"

"No bus."

"I know that tour by heart. *On the right we see…*"

We look at each other and laugh.

An interesting thing happens as I walk along the streets of Palermo. With my feet on the ground, I sense a current running through the city that I hadn't felt from the top of the bus. I'd been so focused on finding the tourist spots that I almost missed the heartbeat of Palermo, but it's all around me. It's a woman lighting a candle in a humble church, a waitress navigating a language barrier to serve us lunch, a vendor hawking his wares at the market. It's Sicilian people with a rich history and a passion for life that give this city an unmistakable spirit and vibrancy. Seen this way, the city becomes much more interesting.

On a side street, a woman stands in her doorway and shouts to a man on a scooter. Her words are loud and punctuated with many hand gestures. In Sicily, the beautiful, flowing Italian language I love has another face, and I've learned that in informal situations, some Sicilians may use a dialect with no direct Italian translation. Perhaps the woman is saying: *When you get to the store, love, please don't forget eggs for the carbonara. Ciao!* (Blows a kiss.) But with Sicilian passion it sounds like: *If you ever do that again I will cut off your head and turn it into a flowerpot!* (Rude hand gesture.) The man on the scooter zooms off.

# Lost at Sea
## *Disperso in Mare*

The Mediterranean Sea. On our first day in Italy, it teased me with flashes of sapphire, playing peek-a-boo on our drive from Naples to Sorrento. While sipping limoncello at Bruno's lemon farm, we heard stories of sailors who crossed from the Middle East to bring the first lemon trees to Italy. I spent an entire day in its company along the Amalfi Coast and journeyed on a ferry as its waters turned from Italian to Sicilian. I was so close, so very close to touching it.

Today is the day.

While waiting in the lobby for our driver, I pull the folded paper out of my purse and re-read the itinerary: *Cefalù is a charming, small city, home to a preserved Medieval cathedral, restaurant-packed old town, fabulous beach and more. Just an hour from Palermo, it's a worthy stop on any trip through Sicily.*

A beach. A *fabulous beach* no less.

Our driver arrives on time and we chat.

"You will love Cefalù. My family and I drive there often on the weekends," he says.

The word *family* stands out in my mind. On the train ride from Naples, we'd passed some spots along the coast where families were changing in and out of bathing suits alfresco. Anne and I had decided not to bring bathing suits. I would be content to kick off my sandals and walk along the shore in my new turquoise sun dress.

A short ride takes us out of Palermo into the charming seaside village. It looks exactly like the pictures. Amber and terra cotta buildings with rust-colored tile roofs cling to the hillside. Shops and restaurants line the boardwalk along a slender strip of beach. I lift my gaze to the sparkling azure water stretching out as far as I can see, and I am breathless.

"How long do you want to stay? One hour? Two hours?" our driver asks as he pulls into a parking spot. This surprises us. We thought this was a day-long tour.

"Oh, we were hoping to stay longer," Anne replies.

"OK, two hours then. I will see you at 12:00."

And with that, our driver leaves us in the parking lot. We must use our time wisely.

"What do you want to do first, tour the village or..." Ed begins, but I am already heading towards my destination. The scent of sea air calls me.

While Scott and Ed watch from the boardwalk, Anne and I slip off our shoes and wiggle our toes in the warm, soft sand. The beach at Cefalù is crescent-shaped, offering protection from the more aggressive waves and undertow of the Mediterranean. Families gather under umbrellas or lounge on a patchwork of towels spread across the sand. Children make castles, and shriek when wayward waves break down the walls of their creations. The water is dotted with people, some swimming, some standing waist deep, bouncing over the swell of unbroken waves.

I step in and feel my feet sink into the place where water kisses the shore. Gentle waves swirl around my ankles with a wash of white foam, then disappear, pulling the sea back into itself. I turn my face to the horizon and feel the warmth of the sun. There it is. The magical place where the ocean and sky blend into one expanse of aquamarine. No beginning, no end. I stand for several moments—my friends, the tourists, the buzz of the village fade away and I am alone with the sea, the sky, the world.

"There are the guys!" Anne motions to Ed and Scott, bringing me back to the present.

They wave, but aren't enticed to join us. I pull my phone out of my dress pocket, and in a click, I capture a priceless moment.

"Let's walk on the beach for a while," I say.

"I love this! We should have brought our bathing suits," Anne says.

"I know. Here we are, two women who were afraid to wear sundresses, now wishing we were in bathing suits." I laugh while we splash ankle deep along the shore.

Suddenly, my breath catches in my throat. Something is wrong. My stomach lurches and my hand flies to my pocket.

"Anne! My phone is gone!"

"No! Check your purse, maybe you put it in there."

We stop and I search through my purse several times. Nothing. I pat my pocket again and notice, for the first time how shallow it is. The other pocket is flat too. Now panic sets in.

"Oh, Anne! It's gone."

"Okay, okay. We haven't gone too far, let's backtrack. Where did you last use it?"

"The selfie, by the stone steps where we first got into the water."

"See, it's not that far. Let's look."

Anne is my anchor, and I cling to her calm voice. She's right; it couldn't have been gone more than a moment or two. If I can retrieve it from the water quickly... We retrace our steps, our eyes darting over the shallow water. But gentle waves that charmed me moments ago are now predators, poised to drag my phone out to sea.

"What color is it?" Anne asks.

"It's gray with white flowers, but that is only if it landed face down. If it landed face up..."

"Yeah, it's the color of wet sand, but maybe it will shine, like it's reflecting the sun."

We continue to walk, stopping now and then to check out any promising shape or glimmer, but we only find phone-shaped rocks or sunlight playing in the shallow water. Now a fresh fear overtakes me.

"Anne, what if someone took it out of my pocket or purse? You know what those ladies on the train said about Palermo."

"I thought about that, but I'm sure there was no one close by. We would have heard them splashing along behind us."

I hope, oh I hope she's right. By now we are back where I'd taken the last photo. We scour the sand with our eyes, walking in circles from the shore to knee depth while the water grabs the hems of our dresses. It's no use. We trudge up the steps. Ed and Scott have watched our erratic behavior from a distance. When we tell them what happened everyone goes silent. Ed gives me a worried look.

"I'm going back on the beach to keep looking. Maybe someone saw it and picked it up. There's no reason for all of us to hang out here," I say.

Scott and Anne hesitate, but I wave them off.

"Go on."

Ed stays but doesn't walk on the beach with me. He is concerned that someone has stolen my phone, and he wants to research our options. With a knot in my stomach, I walk along the shore retracing my path. I know it's pointless, but I have to give it one more try. How could I have been so careless? My phone. My photos. My online travel journal. What feels like an enormous chunk of my life—gone. And now, according to my husband, this is a security risk. Out of desperation I retrace my steps once more.

"*Parla Inglese*?" I ask the people I meet, they only stare or shrug. Finally, I find an English couple playing in the sand with their two young children, and I explain my situation.

"Oh, my GOD!" The woman exclaims. "How can you be so calm? I would freak OUT if I lost my phone!"

I am. She can't see the tears that I'm blinking back behind my sunglasses.

"Perhaps if you ask at the ice cream shop," the man points up the street. "This is a family friendly beach. If someone has found it, they might have turned it in. We'll keep our eyes out for it."

I thank the couple and venture further down the beach where I find a young man lounging on a blanket under an umbrella. Yes, he speaks English. He's Australian, he tells me. He works on one of the cruise ships and has come to the beach on his day off. After hearing my story, he offers some tech savvy advice.

"Is your phone a newer model?"

"Yes, I bought it just before we left for our trip."

*Oh man, there's another reason to cry,* I think. We are still paying for it, and no, we opted not to purchase the insurance because I wasn't planning on tossing my new phone into the ocean.

"Well, the newer models are waterproof for a while. If you find it soon, you might salvage it. Now, if it gets washed ashore and someone picks it up, you have some time to deactivate it because the thief would have to dry it out in rice and could not get to your data for several hours."

The thought of someone drying out my phone in rice before stealing my information only adds to my despair.

I plod back to the stairs and meet up with Ed. He couldn't track my phone, but he was able to deactivate it. So, there is that.

"I want to try one more thing," I say.

"What?"

"The people I talked to said I should ask at the ice cream shop. Someone might have turned it in."

Ed is skeptical, but agrees to try. I can't find the ice cream shop, but I see a woman setting up her cafe for lunch.

"Closed," she says when I approach.

"*Parla Inglese?*" I ask. "I've lost my phone. *Telephono.*" I pantomime holding a cell phone.

"No." She frowns, irritated that I have interrupted her, then calls a young man from the back.

We attempt to communicate, but without my translator app, it's difficult. Finally, the man hands me his phone and shows that I should type in my situation.

As he reads, he nods.

"No phone here. Police station." He points to a two-story white building across the street.

"*Grazie, grazie,*" I say.

Four young Italian police officers stand in the doorway, laughing and smoking cigarettes as Ed and I approach. When I ask if anyone speaks English, one officer smirks, then yells for someone inside. Soon an older, more substantial officer comes to the door and I repeat my sad story.

"I was wondering if anyone turned in a cell phone?"

"No, Madame, no phones."

He dismisses me with a wave of his hand, and I swear, I can hear the officers laughing at me behind my back. *Another crazy American tourist who has lost her precious cell phone. You think we have nothing better to do? Come back when you have a murder to report.*

It's almost time for us to meet our driver. Hoping to cheer me up, Ed suggests gelato. Neither of us speak as we sit on the curb to wait for Anne and Scott. Gelato usually boosts my spirits, but this isn't gelato—it's Italian ice, and the frozen lemon concoction leaves a bitter taste in my mouth.

While we were searching for my phone, our friends explored the city of Cefalù. They'd done some sightseeing and found some real gelato. I can tell they want to gush about it, but are sensitive to the fact the day had not gone according to plan for me and are reserved with their comments. I love them for that. The drive home is somber.

After a quick lunch we go back to the hotel to rest and regroup. Using Ed's phone, I call my children to let them know my phone is out of commission and if they get a call, it will most likely be from a fish at the bottom of the Mediterranean—or a thief. My practical, techie son walks us through an app that would locate my phone, just in case someone has picked it up. Because Ed has deactivated the account, my phone is not traceable.

The call to my daughter is unsettling.

"Mom, please tell me you're not one of those people who save their passwords on their phone in a folder marked passwords.... OH, MOM!"

I spend our last afternoon in Palermo in the hotel room, using Ed's phone to log into all of my accounts to change the passwords. I'm still upset, but this is our last night in Sicily. I take a long shower and dress for dinner. Picking up my purse I notice the empty spot inside where I *used* to keep my phone. We meet Anne and Scott and walk out of the hotel to find a restaurant. On the way, a couple pulls over to the side of the road and asks Ed for directions. They think he's Italian. It's the hat and the shorts and the untucked white shirt with the sleeves rolled up. He plays the part perfectly and directs them somewhere. It's hilarious.

We find an outdoor cafe that has just opened for dinner. As usual, we are early by Italian standards. The main dinner crowd won't show up for several more hours, but it's a lovely setting, and the menu looks inviting. We order drinks and toast to Sicily and Palermo, to hop on busses that we can't wait to get off of, and to phones at the bottom of the sea. I manage a smile, but while the others rave about their meals, my pasta is undercooked.

As we are getting ready for bed, all the emotions I'd been holding in come bursting out. This was supposed to be MY day. The best day ever. Walking in the sea was a bucket list item. I dissolve into tears. This doesn't happen often and when it does, my husband does not know what to do. This time he simply holds me and lets the tears come. When I've used up all the Kleenex, he gets another box from the bathroom and sits on the bed beside me.

"It's ok. It's ok..." he says.

Once I've sniffed my last sniffle, I know he's right. Out of all the catastrophes that could befall a traveler—illness, accident, emergency back home—it's just a phone. I can let this experience ruin the rest of my trip, or suck it up and move on.

I choose to move on.

Tomorrow, we leave Sicily and my phone behind and head for the last leg of our trip. Venice is calling.

*I'm sorry, Deb's not able to answer her phone right now. Leave a message after the.... blub ...blub.... blub...*

# Venice

*Perhaps it is because Venice is both liquid and solid,
both air and stone, that it somehow combines all the
elements crucial to make our imaginations ignite
and turn fantasies into realities.*
*~ Erica Jong*

# Return to Venice
## Ritornare a Venezia

Our driver navigates through the deserted, early-morning streets of Palermo, quite a contrast from the congested traffic we'd experienced on our hop-on bus tour a few days ago. We reach the airport on the outskirts of town in plenty of time. It's a good thing because there are long lines forming at the luggage check and a mob of people going through security. Travelers jostle for position while being funneled towards narrow roped-off lanes. Ed is tall and has a knack for moving through crowds. He holds my hand as we plow through. Scott and Anne are less aggressive and we lose sight of them momentarily, but we all end up on the right plane at the right time.

I settle into my seat and prepare for the first leg of a two-flight trip. The plane is small, a 'puddle jumper' Ed calls it. We are compatible seat mates. I take the window seat to watch the scenery and Ed prefers the aisle, so he can have more leg room. This flight takes us across the water from Palermo to Rome. After take-off, I raise the window shade and view the vast Mediterranean glittering pink in the sunrise as we leave Sicily, and my phone, behind. I'm still tender over my loss. Fortunately, I'd packed a journal in my carry-on. I pull it out and words I didn't, or couldn't say last night, tumble across the page.

This morning, I reached to the nightstand; then I remembered. I couldn't check the time or my social media accounts or the online journal I'd been taking notes in. A ridiculous amount of my life was on that phone. Hopefully, most will be recoverable. I will probably miss the camera most—documenting this trip in photos was important to me as a writer, blogger, and traveler. During my meltdown last night, Ed assured me I could use his phone, but it won't be the same. I'll have to ask, and he'll have to dig it out of his pocket and I know it will make him nervous. It will hamper my spontaneity, but I'll manage. This incident is only a blip in the vacation. Maybe it will make a funny story someday. Not now.

It's a fifty-minute plane trip to Rome, and soon we are preparing for our second flight. It seems unreal that we were at this airport ten days ago. We take a bus from our gate to the tarmac where our plane to Venice is waiting. Flight crews roll stairs up to the plane and we board like movie stars. I turn and wave before I step into the plane. The paparazzi are not interested.

But they should be.

We are stars returning to Venice for our second act. Our foursome visited the city of canals the first time we toured Italy and were so enamored, we wanted to end this trip with an encore. During that first trip we also experienced Milan, Florence, and Rome, all magnificent in their own right, but nothing compared to the charms of Venice.

I will never forget stepping out of the train station onto the banks of the Grand Canal. Of course I'd seen pictures, but this, this took my breath away. The patina of centuries-old buildings contrasted with the brilliant blue sky, while gondolas and motor boats paraded past the copper dome of the Chiesa San Simeone Piccolo. I was in love.

Today, our pilot announces that cool and windy weather is heading towards Venice and to expect a turbulent flight. The sign on the seat in front of me reads: *Fasten seat belt while seated*. When spoken in English, the directive is straightforward and serious, each word punctuated with consonant sounds. The sentence ends with a thud. The end. Do it. Period. However, when the flight attendant reads this same announcement in Italian, *Mantenere le cinture allacciate quando seduti*, the sentence dances in my ears and ends on an up-note with a slight sigh suggesting there might be more to the story. Yes, of course...I will do this. I can't wait to fasten my seatbelt, in fact, let us all put on our seatbelts and then we will celebrate with a glass of sparkling Prosecco! *Salute* to the seatbelts!

The Prosecco, of course is a figment of my imagination, yet we land safely at Marco Polo Airport. We had agreed to pay the extra fare for a private water taxi to take us to our hotel, but due to the turbulent weather, lightweight water taxis are not running today. Disappointed, we purchase tickets for the more substantial water bus to shuttle us across.

It's windy, cool and rainy as we wait on the crowded dock for our turn. I dig through my suitcase, pull out a sweater and rain jacket, and put both on. Finally, we board the water bus and squeeze into seats in the covered cabin. It's a rocky ride across the bay, and we bump across angry gray waves catching glimpses of the muddled landscape through fogged-up, plastic windows. The Italian flag on the back of the boat snaps and snarls at us. This was not the grand welcome to Venice I had been dreaming about.

When we enter the city, things look better. In the shelter of the canals, the water is calm, and the wind subdued. We see a few groups of tourists, but it looks as if the weather has thinned out the crowds. This will be to our advantage.

"If we get off at the Rialto Bridge, I can navigate us to our hotel. I learned how to read the signs before," Ed says.

I remember how difficult it had been to navigate on our last visit, but Ed had figured it out by the time we left. This time, he was confident, and I had no reason to doubt him.

When the water bus stops at the Rialto, we climb out with our luggage. It is still chilly and gray, but the rain has slowed to a light mist. As a back-up navigator, Anne has googled directions from the bridge to the Santa Maria, "*a small boutique hotel just a five-minute walk from the Rialto,*" the listing reads. But, once again, Venice plays tricks on us.

This floating city connects through a series of waterways—canals that spread out like fingers. It has no cars, only boats. What is left behind are narrow footpaths whose names, if they even have names, change frequently as they meander between withering buildings. This, of course, is the charm of Venice, what tourists come to see, yet GPS systems and googled directions make no sense here. It isn't long before we are in trouble. Ed is relying on visual memories from several years ago, and Anne is trying to navigate from her phone's walking GPS directions which show an image of a tiny man following a series of blue dots through a maze of streets. Every time she stops and turns to look at something, the little man has to re-calibrate. And so do we.

Usually an amicable team, Ed and Anne are now at odds. Ed's directions conflict with Anne's, and neither is getting us where we need to be. Scott and I offer many *helpful* suggestions, but this only adds to the confusion. Our 'five-minute walk' turns into an hour and we still haven't found our hotel. To make matters worse, the romantic bridges that crisscross the canals become nightmares when pulling luggage. Ed has both of our suitcases and he is thumping them up and down the steps as he becomes more and more frustrated.

In the life of every vacation, even well-planned ones, there comes a point when the mood shifts from having fun to... not so much. Sometimes it comes out of the blue; sometimes, it's a combination of a series of events—like say, you lose your phone, and Venice is ugly today, and you are hungry and lost, and your husband is destroying your luggage—and you get to a "last straw" moment.

This, is that moment.

"Quit dragging those bags up the steps. You're going to knock the wheels off," I snap.

"Fine! I'll carry them."

Ed stops mid-stride, collapses the telescoping handle on each bag and hoists them, one in each hand, as he hunches over and plods along.

Mild-mannered Anne, uncomfortable with the outburst and not one to cause a scene, quietly pockets her phone and lets Ed take the lead. We lumber in stormy silence through several more dead ends and backtracks.

Just when I think all is lost, we make the right turn into the right courtyard and there it is. The two-story, yellow structure with green shutters and flower boxes—Hotel Santa Maria is a welcome sight. Our travel agent had originally booked us into an expensive hotel right on the Grand Canal, but we opted for a local establishment off the tourist trail. I am questioning our choice—would we ever be able to find it again? —but it is charming. The small lobby is filled with quaint Venetian furniture: velvet tufted chairs with gold accents, petite armoires, a marble topped desk. The clerk checks us in and the bellhop escorts us up and down a series of small staircases and hallways until we come to two small rooms on the bottom floor. We have this wing of the hotel to ourselves.

"Let me show you the shortcut," he says. "Look."

He shows us a private entrance that our room keys can access to outdoors.

"Now you do not need to come through the hotel."

We thank our escort and separate into our own rooms, agreeing to meet in an hour to get something to eat. To be honest, we need a break from each other.

Exhausted, I flop down on the bed and close my eyes, attempting to ward off a headache. Ed explores the room, then pulls back the draperies.

"Deb, you've got to see this!" he says.

"I just want to lie here," I grumble, putting my arm across my eyes. I really don't want to see him or anything else.

"Come on!" He takes my hand and leads me to the window.

I am speechless.

Our room is on water level with a small canal, and waves lap gently at the side of the building. If the water was two feet higher, it would come in the window. Just then, the ornately carved tip of a gondola glides past. A young couple snuggles close on a plush red bench while the gondolier stands on the back of his boat in his iconic black-and-white striped shirt and jaunty cap. He navigates by pulling the oar through the water in strong, sure strokes and is so close to our window, I could reach out and touch him. The rain has stopped and the late afternoon sun streams through the window. Ed hands me his phone.

"You're going to want a picture of this."

And just like that, Venice returns to me.

# Tourists
## *Turisti*

*Venice, the most touristy place in all the world,*
*is still just completely magic to me.*
*~ Frances Mayes*

The canal that charmed me yesterday with the iconic gliding gondola, has another life. During the night, motorboats puttered by our window blaring Italian pop music. It seems our hotel is adjacent to a teenager's cruising route. Picture a fifty's diner scene, but with boats. In the morning, the spot we thought was a private patio outside of our rooms, is in fact a busy loading dock where boats deliver goods and pick up trash and laundry for the hotel. Across the canal, a building is undergoing construction. It's fascinating to see supplies and equipment coming down the canal on barges and workers balancing on boats to get what's needed up and into the construction site. Despite its allure, Venice is a working, breathing city that supports locals who in turn support the throngs of tourists who flock here. Because we've been to this city before, and we make our own plans, I like to think we are a bit savvier than the mass of people breakfasting in the hotel dining room who will soon traipse through the city as part of a large group.

Still, today we are tourists.

"I've got my bearings now," Ed says as we leave the hotel.

And he's right. The signs on the side of the buildings make sense. All arrows point to one of two spots: the Rialto Bridge or San Marco Square. This morning we are going towards the square. Yesterday's gray skies have vanished, the beautiful weather lifts my spirits, and as promised, Ed leads with confidence. The piazza is alive with vendors setting up their carts and cafe workers arranging tables and chairs to welcome early guests. A long line has already formed for St. Mark's Basilica, one of Venice's most popular attractions.

Having toured the Basilica on our previous trip, we have decided to visit the Doge's Palace today. Anne and Scott enjoy historical sites and this was on their 'must see' list. While we wait to purchase tickets, it occurs to me I don't know what a Doge is or what we are waiting in line to see. Scott informs me.

"A Doge is like an Italian duke. Whoever held this office was the highest official of the republic of Venice."

"So, this would have been his home?" I ask.

"One of his residences, and it served as a center of government."

Who needs a guide when you have Scott? We don our earbuds and set off on a self-guided tour beginning in the grand courtyard. Don't get me wrong, I am fascinated by the history of Venice, but all the dates and personalities confuse me. Instead of a textbook history lesson, I focus on small details of the tour. What speaks to me? What stories will I keep?

I am immediately drawn to the grand stairway in the courtyard. During the fifteenth century, the Great Council of Venice decided the palace needed a single monumental entrance from the piazza. The Giant's Stairway is a beautiful stone and marble structure guarded at the top by two colossal statues of Mars and Neptune by the Italian Renaissance sculptor Jacopo Sansovino. The stairway would impress visiting dignitaries and remind them of Venice's power by land and sea as the two gods glared down at them.

Inside the palace, I'm excited to see the famous Scala d'Oro (Golden Staircase), though disappointed to learn it isn't really made of gold. The voice coming through my earbuds says it was named for the elaborate decorations in white and gold stucco that adorn the arched ceiling. I'm thinking a real gold staircase would have made a bigger statement from the Doge—I'm sure he could have afforded it—yet the climb is impressive nonetheless. Once only illustrious visitors were allowed, but today, tourists in shorts and flip-flops ascend the magnificent staircase that leads to the Doge's apartments. We can't go into the private rooms, but there's a public bathroom on this floor for our convenience. Having learned our lesson of never passing up a free bathroom in Italy, Anne and I join the long line of women moving slowly due to the bathroom attendant guarding the door. As one person exits, the matron inspects the recently vacated stall and sink area before letting another woman in. The Doge must have had high standards of cleanliness.

This same wing of the palace houses impressive state rooms where the senate and council met, as well as rooms where criminals faced justice. Our audio-tour directs us to another set of stairs. In contrast to the abundance and grandeur of the upper floors, we now descend a narrow cave-like staircase into the prison cells that were built to house those awaiting trial. Once convicted, officials would lead prisoners through the notorious Bridge of Sighs, a corridor passing from the courtrooms to the prison cells. Designed with small windows facing the lagoon, they supposedly named it after the sound the prisoners made when seeing their last glimpse of freedom. The Doge's palace seems a dichotomy to me—art and majesty above and prisons below— yet one can't deny the time-capsule of Venice it represents.

Full to the brim with history, we exit the Palace and enter San Marco Square to find tourists have taken over. They flock to the stands to buy souvenirs—magnets, hats, tee-shirts, key chains, and other trinkets—while high-end shops that border the square sell items for the more discriminating taste. Café workers have draped their tables in white while musicians perform for their patrons. The center of the plaza is packed with wanna-be fashion models and TikTok influencers posing for pictures. Ed has an idea.

"Let have lunch here!"

"I understand the gin and tonics are outstanding." Scott grins.

"Oh, no you don't," says Anne

It's a running joke, one of our collective travel tales that gets embellished with each repetition. On our first visit to Venice, Anne and I left the guys in the square while we went shopping. They sat at a cafe and ordered drinks, delighted that they also received a complimentary bowl of potato chips. It was a hot day; the chips were salty, and the gin and tonics disappeared quickly. Maybe a bit too quickly, as it resulted in a lapse of judgment.

"Another round for you?" the server asked.

Of course. The empty glasses disappeared, and two more drinks and another bowl of chips arrived. By the time Anne and I arrived, our guys were in a good mood.

"What are you doing?" Anne asks.

"Just having a drink while waiting for our lovely wives to join us," Scott says.

"I heard the drinks here are really expensive. Did you check the prices?"

"No, but the chips are free."

We should have known better, but Anne and I ordered drinks. When the bill came, our husbands were quick to pick up the receipts. At her insistence Scott handed their tab to Anne. She raised her eyebrows and gave him a look that said "I told you so." Ed shoved our tab in his pocket, and to this day, I have no idea what we spent that afternoon. I'm happier not knowing because in my mind, it was worth it. We can say we had drinks at an elegant table in San Marco Square. Once.

This time we decide to step out of the stream of tourists and find a cozy outdoor cafe in a quieter, more reasonably priced part of town. Ed and I share a pizza topped with Parma ham and mozzarella. The pizzas in Venice differ from the traditional pizzas in Naples. The tomato sauce is thicker and you have more choices of toppings. It's still nothing like the loaded American pizzas, yet we are learning to appreciate the simple taste of fresh, local ingredients. We share thoughts about our morning adventure over glasses of wine while finishing our lunch.

"I can't get over the Doge's Palace," Scott says. "In Shakespeare's *Othello*, the opulence of 16th century Venice is described. Now I can picture it."

"This is why we travel: to experience the world, see things we've only read about, experience something different than our everyday lives." Anne adds.

It's late afternoon now and the lines of tourists make the narrow walking paths between the building nearly impossible. Tour guides hold up flags and struggle to keep track of their groups. It's easy to spot Ed's Italian fedora over the crowds; however, he is like a bloodhound on the scent of the trail, watching for street signs and moving ahead with nothing but his next destination in mind. Anne and I like to wander and stop to window shop which causes us to lag. When this happens, Scott takes the role of a nervous sheepdog trying to keep his flock together. He paces between Ed and us, trying to keep both parties in sight.

"Ed, Ed, the girls have stopped back there," he shouts.

"What?"

"We've lost the girls."

"Where?"

"I think they stopped at the gelateria."

Our husbands turn and backtrack to find Anne and I motioning to them.

"We need some gelato," I say.

"The line is too long, it will take forever," Ed says.

He's right. The hit-and-run tourists have bolted off the cruise ships and with limited time at their disposal, are eager to experience gelato, the holy grail of Italian delights. It is one of the most touristy things to do in Venice.

"But gelato...," I whine pointing to the people leaving the shop. Their large waffle cones overflow with mounds of creamy goodness and are topped with a signature wafer. Irresistible.

Ed gives in. It's three to one, and he knows this is a battle he will not win. Besides, who can say no to gelato? We take our place in line as it inches along. This gives me time to plan my selections. This time I go all out and order three scoops—*cioccolato* (chocolate), *stracciatella* (creamy vanilla with chocolate shavings), and *dulce de leche* (caramel). In a waffle cone. With a wafer on top.

With our towering treats in hand, we start back to the hotel. On a picturesque bridge that crosses one of the lesser canals, a crowd is growing. We find a place to stand along the railing to finish our gelato. A masquerade in progress!

When traveling in Venice, you can't help but notice shops that sell or rent elaborate masks and costumes. In our tour through the Doge's palace, I discovered that the tradition of masquerade is part of the city's history. Venice has always been a thriving center of trade and a tourist destination attracting people from all over the world. During certain times of the year, the ruling Doge would allow carnivals where Venetians and foreigners, men and women, rich and poor could mingle as equals behind masks and costumes. Masquerade balls still occur in the city.

Today a young couple is posing for a photo shoot on the bridge. The woman is tall and slender, the perfect frame to showcase the gossamer, golden cape that flows over her long black gown. She wears a glittering black mask that covers most of her face. Her headdress is a spectacular display of black feathers, and silver bobbles dangle from her ears. She stands silent, regal, mysterious. Her partner is costumed as a jester. He wears a black shirt with pants that are cropped at the knees and standing in bare feet, he appears much shorter than the woman. To complete the comic effect, a golden coil forms his crown and similar pieces form a collar and cuffs. A simple gold mask surrounds his eyes.

A photographer stands by to adjust costumes and offer directions. The iconic canal makes a perfect backdrop, and he positions the couple on the bridge just so, in order to take advantage of the rose-colored afternoon light. They dance and twirl as he captures them in motion. Now and then, they stop, and peer into the camera to approve or disapprove the shots. The photographer is patient. He continues to make adjustments and take pictures until they are satisfied with the fantasy they've created. I am spellbound.

When the masquerade ends, I clap my gelato-sticky hands to join fellow tourists in applause. The queen and her jester bow and make a grand exit down the stairs, then disappear into the crowd. This then, is Venice.

Touristy? Of course.

Completely magical? Without a doubt.

# My Way
## *A Modo Mio*

In order to find a more intimate way to see Venice, we sign up for a walking tour to sample local cuisine and signature drinks. We arrive at the plaza in front of the Basilica Giovanni a few minutes early and find a seat along the canal to wait for our tour guide.

"Look at those kids," Scott says.

I glance over to see neighborhood kids kicking a soccer ball into the side of the basilica. They are using the expanse of the plaza as their court and the stone wall of the church as a goal, ensuring that the soccer ball doesn't end up in the canal. They seem to aim at one particular large stone and cheer when a teammate kicks the ball into it.

"That's a ledger stone marking who is buried within the walls of the church," Scott informs us.

The thought of a poor soul hoping to rest in peace now being thumped by a soccer ball strikes me as funny, though I probably should show more respect. Soon, an attractive young woman carrying a clipboard approaches us. She is wearing casual slacks and a tee shirt. The addition of an oversized blazer (sort of) gives her an air of authority.

"I'm Emma. Are you here for the "Eat like an Italian' tour?" she asks.

We introduce ourselves, and she checks our names on her roster.

"There will be two other couples."

When Scott mentions the soccer game, Emma laughs.

"They've figured out how to make it work here in the square. You've probably noticed there are no soccer fields in the city."

"Do you live in Venice?" Anne asks.

"Yes, I am a student at the university. I grew up in a town not too far from here and spent the summers with my grandmother in Venice. It was a wonderful place to grow up. After breakfast we would leave Grandmother's apartment and have the free run of the city. We would stay out all day playing in the streets and the plazas like this," she points to the children playing soccer. "It's very safe, no cars, and we knew all the neighbors."

"I have to keep reminding myself that Venice isn't only for tourists, that it's a place where people live and work and play and go to school," I say.

"Yes, look," Emma points to a cathedral-like building in front of us. "What do you think this is? A church? A museum? No! It's a hospital. During the tour, we will walk right past the emergency entrance."

By now our group has assembled, and we spend a few moments getting to know each other. Jess and Darius are a young couple from New Jersey. I can already tell Jess is going to be fun. She is wearing a short, white sundress, her tightly braided hair is wound into an elaborate do. Her husband is an accountant and seems more reserved. Our other tour companions Laura and John are on their honeymoon.

"So, we are all here to eat...and drink like Italians, right?" Emma asks, eliciting smiles, nods, and thumbs-ups from the group. "I am going to take you to some of my favorite places, places that locals prefer. All right then? Follow me."

Ironically, we pass our hotel on the way to our first stop. I take comfort in knowing we aren't venturing too far from home base.

"This first stop is a popular place for young people to come after work."

Emma leads us into a tiny pub bustling with activity. We crowd inside and squeeze around two tables. Ed and I find seats next to John and Laura. Emma orders a "shadow" of wine (a short pour) for each of us—our choice of house red or white—and several plates of assorted bruschetta.

"Congratulations on your wedding, and what a great place for a honeymoon," I say to Laura.

"Thanks. We got married in Toronto. That was our official wedding, then our storybook wedding was in France, and now we are on a European tour. What about you guys?" she asks flashing the diamond nugget on her ring finger.

"Forty-eight years," I say flashing mine, though my diamond is more of a spark than a flash. "We're traveling through Italy and Sicily with our good friends." I motion to Scott and Anne at the other table.

"Wow, that's a long marriage," John says. "I've got a lot to live up to."

*Good luck with that buddy,* I think to myself. Not only the number of years, but his new wife has high expectations—storybook wedding, giant diamond, European honeymoon...

After finishing our shadows of wine and bruschetta, we walk a short distance to our next stop, an area I'm familiar with. It's next to the gelato shop we visited yesterday. (I never forget a gelato shop.)

"Now here we will sample one of my favorites, *mozzarella en carrozza,* mozzarella in a carriage. They fill a pocket of Italian bread with fresh mozzarella and perhaps a slice of prosciutto, then pop it in the fryer. When you bite into it, strings of mozzarella stretch out from the sandwich like reins from a carriage. They invented it in this very restaurant and it's perfect for a quick bite when you don't have time for a sit-down meal. Maybe you will have a sip of wine with it?"

Of course, we will.

It's love at first ooey-gooey bite—like an Italian grilled cheese or a gourmet Hot-Pocket. We stand outside and I laugh as I try to manage the strings of mozzarella running down one hand and a glass of wine in the other. The gelateria is so very close...perhaps desert? But sadly, we don't stop there. Instead, we backtrack to the plaza where we started the tour, and this time, follow the canal past the hospital. Here we see ambulance-boats, complete with blue lights and red crosses, moored to the dock at the emergency entrance.

"See, if you eat or drink too much tonight, we are prepared for you," Emma jokes.

I try to imagine being rushed to the hospital in a gondola ambulance. Do you get a cute gondoliere who sings to you while administering CPR? I'd rather not find out. It's a good thing we are on foot between our food and beverage stops. I can tell we will need to walk off our libations. Anne and I join Jess and discover she is originally from Jamaica. She asks about our families and tells us she wants to have lots of kids.

"That's one reason we want to move from Jersey," she says. "We are looking around a for more family friendly and affordable place to raise a family."

We tell her we are retired educators, and Anne mentions I am a writer.

"You four are amazing!" she says. "You're out there doing things, not content to sit back and stay at home. I love it!"

This prompts Anne to tell Jess about our lingerie shopping experience in Sorrento. I chime in when needed, elaborating on the more colorful parts to enhance the effect.

"That's hysterical! I wish I could have seen the look on your face when she held up the thong," she says.

I think maybe this gets our foursome out of the league of "the older couples" and into the category of "fun, interesting, and vibrant" which is exactly the way I feel at the moment. Perhaps it's the wine, and we're not done yet.

We stop at another small pub and Emma offers us a choice of two of Italy's famous aperitifs, Campari and Aperol, made into spritzes by adding prosecco and soda water and served before a dinner to stimulate the appetite.

"Both are similar, but the Aperol is sweeter. Campari has a more bitter taste," she explains.

I immediately go for my favorite. Darius orders a Campari spritz. He takes a sip of his and makes a face.

"Too bitter for me. I should have gone with the Aperol Spritz," he says.

"So, I hear you want lots of kids," I say.

"Well, I ...we... are in negotiations on what 'lots' means," he says glancing at Jess who is engaged in another conversation.

I can see the accountant wheels turning in his head as he swizzles the ice around in his glass.

"How's everyone doing? Did you enjoy your spritzes?" Emma asks. "I have one more place to show you. How about gelato for dessert?"

Hearing no complaints from the group, Emma leads us farther and farther away from our starting point. I'm hoping Ed and Anne are keeping track of our route because I'm lost in the moment. The Venetian sky is streaked with orange and crimson, providing the perfect backdrop for the city's silhouette. I use Ed's phone to take pictures of the sun setting over iconic bridges as gondolas cater to sunset-seeking tourists. Cathedral bells float evening songs on the late summer breeze and my mind drifts away. I'm brought back to the present when we reach our next destination.

"To get the best gelato, you must stay away from the tourist areas. Sometimes those shops sell gelato that is made from mixes, thinking you won't know the difference. It is best to find local shops that make their own. This one is one of the best in Venice and they are famous for their pistachio," Emma tells us.

I look at the case and hesitate. Out of all the alluring choices, the pistachio gelato looks the least appealing. It's a drab olive color and I'm not even sure I like pistachios, yet I'm willing to try. I am not disappointed.

Our group gathers to enjoy our gelato and this last stop on the tour. Far off of the tourist trail, this is a place where young people mix with families to enjoy drinks or dinner items from the local cafes. They sit at dockside tables or lounge on blankets, picnic style, watching the last rays of the sun fade into night. Motor boats cruise up and down the canal, sometimes blaring favorite songs, creating an atmosphere of a party or outdoor concert. We've had a wonderful time. The food and drinks and our young companions have put us in a good mood. Soon Emma will lead us back to our starting point. From there, it will be easy to find our hotel. She looks at her phone.

"I'm meeting my boyfriend here. Are you all OK with getting back on your own?"

Our companions assure her they will be fine, but Scott and I look at each other in desperation. This is not going to end well.

"Do you know the way back?" I whisper to Ed.

"Yeah, I think so."

"Get directions!" I hiss.

We say our goodbyes and while the rest of the group wanders off, Ed asks Emma how to get back to the basilica.

"Oh, sure, sure. It's easy. See this bridge there? Go over it and turn to the right. Go across three more bridges and turn...." her voice goes on and I see Ed and Anne nodding, but my heart sinks. I don't want a repeat of what happened when we were trying to find our hotel on our first day here. We say our goodbyes and barely get over the first bridge before confusion sets in.

"Turn right," Anne says.

Ed hesitates.

"Ok, but this doesn't look right. This is not the way we came. Is that bridge counted as one of the three or do we go across this one here?"

This goes on for a while and to make matters worse, it's dark and the dimly lit streets are deserted. There are no signs or familiar sights for Ed to follow and by now we are far off of Emma's directions. Finally, Anne gets out her phone and calls up Little Blue Walking Man on her GPS. I don't know what is wrong with him, but we follow his line of blue dots around in circles until we run into a dead end where we interrupt an amorous couple in a dark doorway telling each other goodnight.

So, here's the thing. Ed has an excellent sense of direction once he gets his bearings. He relies on visual cues, directional position, and memory. Anne is a great navigator when she has a reliable map. We have none of those tools now. Scott and I, having no sense of direction, are normally content to hang back and go along for the ride. But I'll be damned if I'm going to spend the next several hours wandering around the dark side of Venice. Something wild and powerful and unexpected comes over me. I take charge.

"Give me your phone," I say to Ed.

"Deb, GPS isn't working," he argues.

"Give... me... your... phone."

He digs into his pocket and hands it over.

"Anne, what's the address of our hotel?"

I plug the address into the system and make sure the phone is on walking mode. Instead of Little Blue Walking Man, a solid blue arrow appears on the display. Much better. I've lost all faith in that guy anyway. Holding the phone chest-high and steady, I point the arrow in the direction I'm facing.

"This way," I say.

By this time everyone is so distraught that no one challenges me. I lead the pack with blinders on, my eyes glued to the device I'm holding. The arrow leads us down small streets and pathways, over bridges and under archways. I have no idea where we are and nothing looks familiar. *Please, oh PLEASE let this work* I think, but I hold firm and trust the arrow. Within ten minutes, we are back at Hotel Santa Maria.

There is no fanfare. In fact, my monumental accomplishment is hardly acknowledged, but I get into bed and fall asleep with a smile on my face. For the first time in all of our travels, I was the navigator.

And I was good at it.

# Thousand Flowers
## *Millefiori*

Today we plan to venture off the main island of Venice to explore some of the smaller islands. When we were in San Marco square a few days ago, we were approached by several tour guides offering package deals to the islands of Murano, known for its glassware, and Burano where exquisite lace is made. While we were tempted to buy tickets that day, we discovered that it's fairly simple, and much more economical, to plan the trip ourselves and follow our own agenda.

Depending on where you are in Venice, you can navigate to the islands via vaporetti (water buses). Much like a bus system in other large cities, water busses in and around Venice run on a series of lines that crisscross the lagoons. You can also hire a private water taxi, but these are much more expensive. We purchase vaporetti tickets to Murano to begin our adventure.

Ed and I take seats on the floating dock, but Anne and Scott are having a conversation at the ticket booth. Just as the boat arrives, Anne comes dashing onto the dock to inform us that Scott has changed his mind. He's not going.

"He hasn't been feeling well all morning, maybe something he ate or allergies from the hotel room, but he just doesn't feel like getting on a boat and walking around all day."

"So, he's staying?"

"Yeah, I guess. But he insists I go. He doesn't want me to miss out. I really don't think I should leave him. Will he be able to find his way back to the hotel? He doesn't even have a phone."

I can see Scott on the dock waving for us to go on. Anne makes a tough decision. At the last minute, she boards the water bus with Ed and I. As soon as the boat pulls away from the dock, she second-guesses her decision.

"I shouldn't have left him. Oh, man."

She plops down on the seat beside me and puts her head in her hands.

"Anne, he'll be ok. It's not like you are leaving a child. He knows how to take care of himself," I say.

I try to console my friend, but in the back of my mind I am worried. I would feel better if we had a way to keep in touch, but Scott is one who doesn't rely on a phone. He didn't even bring his on the trip with us. Yet, he is in an area with shops and cafes. If he doesn't feel comfortable finding his way back to the hotel, he can sit and wait for us. I'm feeling better about the situation as we leave Venice and

Scott behind and I think Anne is too. At least she is putting up a good front. And she really, really wants to see Murano.

It's a brief ride and after getting our bearings, we find the city's grand canal lined with weathered two storied buildings in shades of terra cotta and umber. Outdoor cafes with colorful awnings and umbrellas invite customers in for a latte or flakey pastry. It is a nice escape from the crowds of Venice and a beautiful day for strolling along the canals and pedestrian bridges that connect the seven small islands of Murano.

We find a glass-blowing shop and watch in awe as the artist sits behind a glass panel and demonstrates his craft. He works with a walnut-sized blob of molten glass at the end of a metal pipe, blowing and spinning it over a small, Bunsen-burner flame until it forms an intricate cup. The showroom is exquisite and the prices reflect the quality of his work.

Further along the canal, we see a group of people gathering outside a warehouse and we investigate. Through the wide-open doors, we observe glass blowing on a larger scale. Several men work on their projects in the large space, while one young man sits in the doorway—apparently, it's his turn to be on display. He twirls a glowing ball of glass on the end of a metal tube while he heats it with a hand-held torch. Now and then he blows into the tube to change the shape of the molten glass, then returns to twirling. Many in the crowd take pictures as the blob takes the form of a vase.

"Look, he's blowing into another tube, a smaller one. I wonder why he's doing that?" a man asks.

Just then, a puff of smoke comes from the glass blower's mouth.

He's vaping. Ancient craft meets modern influences.

Anne wants to see the lighthouse, one of the of the attractions noted in the tourist brochure. The black-and-white striped tower is one of the first things you notice when you come to the city of Murano. It's a working lighthouse and you can't go inside, but it makes an iconic photo backdrop. We find an outdoor café near the water and order lunch.

"I know he's probably back at the hotel by now, but I'm still worried about Scott. Would it be ok with you guys if we skip the trip to Burano and head back after we finish up here?" Anne asks.

Ed and I agree. There are a several more things to see here, and we are both content to cut the lace-making city of Burano. After lunch, we across a bridge and continue sightseeing. A small family shop and studio catches our eye.

"Do you have a glassblowing demonstration?" I ask the woman stocking shelves.

"Oh no Madame, now it is too hot for the fires. We do our glass blowing only in the winter with the cooler temperatures. But I would be happy to take you to our showroom."

While leading us to another part of the building, she explains the process of glassmaking.

"You need to be sure, when you shop you look for authentic Murano glass. When you go to some of the tourist shops, they sell things that are not made in Murano. Look for places like here, family businesses, to find authentic glass. Please, please, take your time. Look around," she says.

Anne is fascinated by a table of miniature, hand-blown glasses.

"Perfect for serving limoncello. Should I get blue or green?"

"One of each," I say.

The woman notices me eying a display of delicate glass pendants.

"You know millefiori?" she asks.

"No, but it's lovely."

"This is an ancient craft. We make it by creating long glass tubes in layers of color, then the rods are heated and pulled thin." The woman stretches her arms wide. "After that, the tubes are cut into cross-sections to make beads for necklaces or placed into designs. When they are heated again, they flatten and form into multi-colored flowers. Millefiori. Thousand flowers."

Thousand flowers. I see them now, in various designs, each unique. I can't take my eyes off the pendant disks where the tiny flowers form a tree. The sales clerk is quick to notice.

"This is a traditional design. Tree of Life. It is for strength, individuality, and rebirth."

My heart skips a beat.

I am not one of those tourists who loads a suitcase with souvenirs, yet on each of our trips, I try to find something that will remind me of where I've been. Despite the sales pitch, the pendant is a perfect symbol of what this trip has been–and will be for me. I select a small one with a black background that shows off the flower tree beautifully. The woman wraps my treasure, and I put it carefully into my purse.

As we leave the shop, I notice a young girl, perhaps five or six years old, walking alone in front of us. I see from her uniform and pink roller bag that she is probably a student heading home after school. She stops to admire the fancy tiaras and glass bead jewelry in a shop window, perhaps imagining treasures that may someday be her own. With dreams of glamor and a toss of her long black hair, she resumes her journey.

It's late afternoon when we board the vaporetto to return to Venice. We chat about our day and visit with a family from Brussels sitting next to us, but as we approach the city, I sense Anne's anxiety mounting. When we dock, she looks for Scott, hoping to see him waiting for us.

He's not here.

With no way to contact him, we hurry back to the hotel. And there he is, in his room reading a book.

"You found your way back! Did you stay here all day? How are you feeling?" Anne says, noticeably relieved.

"Yes, I found my way back, I'm feeling better and it might surprise you to know, that I did not stay here all day. While the maids were cleaning our room, I did some sightseeing. I found a cafe, and a neat stationery shop and a place that sold panini and...what?"

He stops mid-sentence as we stare at him.

Later, walking to dinner, I pull Scott aside.

"You know, I believe they've underestimated us. It appears that you and I are navigators after all."

And I have one more journey to make before saying goodbye to Italy.

# Until We Meet Again
## *Arriverderci*

The first rays of sunlight are sneaking through the curtains. I hope I'm not too late.

"You coming with me?" I ask.

Ed rolls over and looks at his phone. "You're really going to do this?"

"Yep," I say as I pull on yoga pants, tee-shirt and a jacket.

"Ok, yeah, I'm going."

We leave quietly so as not to wake up Anne and Scott in the next room, even though they are aware of my plan. The plaza in front of our hotel is empty. Ed hands me his phone.

"Lead on," he says.

It was a documentary on Venice that put the idea into my head. *You haven't seen Venice until you experience the Rialto Bridge in the early morning before the city wakes up*, the narrator said. For some reason, it stuck with me and, along with walking in the Mediterranean Sea, became one of the two 'must dos' I had for this trip. It's likely I may never experience Venice again in my lifetime. This is my chance to say goodbye.

The streets are quiet as the city slowly wakes up and prepares to greet the throngs that will soon appear. Chairs and tables are stacked and metal roll-down doors cover the store fronts making the tourist thoroughfares unrecognizable. We pass only one business that is open—a coffee shop. I'm tempted to stop in for a latte, but I'm on a mission.

I navigate with confidence, and soon we reach the Rialto. With its central portico flanked by rows of shops, it's one of Venice's most recognizable landmarks and is usually packed with tourists, yet this morning we are alone on the bridge. We walk up the steps and see shuttered shops and a few empty beer bottles—evidence of late-night revelry. The sun breaking over the canal dances on the water, turning the tops of buildings into gold. There are no gondolas out this early, only a few boats ferrying supplies to the hotels. The air is fresh and the sleepy city is quiet. Ed and I stand at the railing and look out over the city as if an artist had created this scene just for us. I take photos, knowing that they won't possibly capture what I'm experiencing at this moment.

"Ready?" Ed whispers.

I nod, reluctant to leave, but I know the bridge will soon fill with tour groups and I don't want to spoil this memory.

"One more thing," I say. "I want to go to San Marco Square."

"I don't know if we have time. We're meeting Scott and Anne for breakfast."

But I've already put it into the phone's navigation system.

"A five-minute walk. We can do it." Without giving him time to protest, I start off.

This is even more amazing. The enormous square, usually packed with tourists and vendors, is almost empty except for a couple pulling their luggage, a young woman in jeans, tee shirt, and bridal veil doing a photo shoot, and three young people taking videos of themselves doing cartwheels. A few rosy clouds float across the blue sky and the rising sun is painting the facade of St Mark's Basilica with streaks of gold. I run across the vast, square, startling early morning pigeons.

"Take my picture, take my picture," I yell back at Ed.

I throw by arms wide, a tiny figure against the backdrop of the majestic Basilica, embracing Venice in all its morning glory.

We return in plenty of time for breakfast, then our foursome heads out for one last day of sightseeing and window shopping. We visit the Museum of Modern Art, leather shops, a beautiful stationery shop that I wished I could have spent more time in and, of course, pizza for lunch.

In the evening, we pack up and meet Anne and Scott for drinks and snacks at the hotel cafe. We raise our glasses in a farewell to Italy.

"*Salute!*"

Anne sighs. "This is why I travel. I can escape my ordinary life, free of my day-to-day responsibilities for a while. I can be an adventurer and see things I've only dreamed of—be my true self. This is what I do for *me.*"

It is a bittersweet moment. We've been on the road for twenty-one days, logged who knows how many miles on planes, trains, boats, and cars, dragged our luggage across Italy and Sicily, slept in many hotel rooms, gained some dresses, lost a phone. Yes, we are ready to go home, and yet, the allure of travel with our close friends tugs at me. It's going to be hard to say goodbye.

"Where to next?" Scott says

"I'm thinking Spain and Portugal," Ed says.

We clink our glasses together—two gin and tonics, one Aperol Spritz, and one Limoncello—and I know we will have barely unpacked our bags before planning our next adventure.

The next morning, a large tour group packs into the dining room before departing. We had passed the hotel staff maneuvering mountains of luggage off the loading dock onto barges that will take their bags to buses on the mainland so their charted tour can continue. Our departure should be much simpler. We have splurged on a private water taxi that will pick us up at the dock only steps from our hotel rooms and transport us across the lagoon to the airport.

When the time comes, our driver maneuvers up to the dock, carefully stows our bags at the bow, then helps us onboard. The dark wood paneled interior and deep blue upholstered seats are lovely, but when our driver maneuvers through the canals I stand at the back of the boat. As we move into the major waterway, I see other taxis arriving and departing— carrying tourists who are leaving Venice and those just beginning their adventures.

I arrived in Italy with antacids, aspirin, and Band-Aids; I leave with a limoncello baptism and a "thousand flowers." I brought black slacks and hiking shirts; I leave with sundresses in orange and turquoise and Italian lace. I came clutching my cellphone; I leave with open arms.

As Venice fades into the distance, the red, white, and green Italian flag flaps behind the boat waving goodbye. I thought two trips to Italy would be enough, now I'm not so sure.

*Arrivederci, Italia.* UNTIL we meet again.

# Epilogue

It's late when we arrive home. I wait until morning to check, afraid of the void I might face. My computer, contrary after being left alone for so many days, takes forever to load. I hold my breath and watch the icon spinning, spinning...and yes! Thanks to technical wonders and the mystical cloud, it's all here! My notes, my pictures—nothing has been lost!

Except that last selfie. It didn't have time to escape to the cloud before my phone landed in the sea. But it doesn't matter. The picture is etched forever in my mind. There I am, standing in the Mediterranean with water lapping my toes. I'm wearing a turquoise sundress and standing where the land becomes water, and behind me the ocean becomes sky. I'm laughing as the sea spray kisses my face, and life fills me to the brim.

There will be several days of jet-lag ahead, and I'll need time to process these past few weeks, but the pictures, the words, the stories—oh, the stories— are already playing in my mind.

I exhale a gentle, slow breath.
Air escaping a bubble.

# Acknowledgements

Writing is a solitary act, but to be a writer you must have a community behind you. This work could not have been completed without the support and encouragement of the members of the Oro Valley Writer's Forum. Through meeting with this group of writers each month for many years I found the courage to become a writer.

Special thanks to my beloved critique group friends: David, Devi, Karen, and Brad. You continue to challenge me to bring forth my best, over cups of coffee and tea, tears...and laughter exactly when needed. (To the point that I fear our *Write Stuff* group runs the risk of being banned from several local coffee shops.)

And to Elizabeth for your friendship and guidance.

What a treasure it is to have these people in my life who are good friends, and great writers.

# About the Author

Debra VanDeventer is a former educator who now channels her creative energies into writing. Her style can best be described as creative nonfiction as small moments bloom into words. In addition to *Until Italy: A Traveler's Memoir,* she is the author of *Out of the Crayon Box: Thoughts on Teaching, Retirement and Life.* Her stories have appeared in *The Desert Leaf* and *Oro Valley Style* magazines and in several anthologies.

Originally from Indiana, Debra has two children and three grandchildren. Along with her husband Ed, she resides in Arizona where life in the desert never ceases to amaze and inspire her. To learn more, visit her blog at **seamslikeastory.com**

Made in the USA
Las Vegas, NV
05 December 2024

13421309R00129